OUTRIGHT
BARBAROUS

To DARRYL and MARYLIN:
Keep fighting!

best,

Jeff

ALSO BY JEFFREY FELDMAN

Framing the Debate: Famous Presidential Speeches and How Progressives Can Use Them To Change The Conversation (And Win Elections)

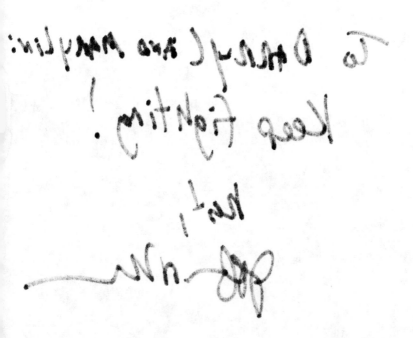

OUTRIGHT
BARBAROUS

HOW THE VIOLENT LANGUAGE OF THE RIGHT POISONS AMERICAN DEMOCRACY

JEFFREY FELDMAN

Brooklyn, New York

Please direct inquiries to:

Ig Publishing
178 Clinton Avenue
Brooklyn, NY 11205
www.igpub.com

Library of Congress Cataloging-in-Publication Data

Feldman, Jeffrey.
  Outright barbarous : how the violent language of the Right poisons American
democracy
/ Jeffrey Feldman.
      p. cm.
  ISBN-13: 978-0-9788431-5-1
  ISBN-10: 0-9788431-5-0
  1. Conservatism--United States. 2. Communication in politics--United
States.
  3. Communication--Political aspects--United States. 4. Journalism--Political
aspects--United
States. 5. Press and politics--United States. 6. Violence--United States. 7.
United States--Politics and government--2001- I. Title.
  JC573.2.U6F44 2008
  320.520973--dc22
                                    2008009370

To my parents

ACKNOWLEDGEMENTS

Reading violent language is an exhausting and at times disheartening task that cannot be done without support from countless people.

The initial seed for *Outright Barbarous* was a short essay I wrote for my blog Frameshop in March of 2007 titled "D'Souza and the Violent Right." It was subsequently republished on *The Huffington Post* and on *Daily Kos*, eliciting forthright and engaging online discussions. I am grateful to all the readers who challenged me with their comments and questions to go deeper into the enormity of the problem explored in that brief post.

Distracted by elections, teaching, and the daily grind of political writing, I would not have completed this book save for the constant encouragement of Robert Lasner and Elizabeth Clementson at Ig Publishing.

I tip my cap to George Lakoff, Glenn Smith, and all my "framing" colleagues at The Rockridge Institute. My study of language in the media and politics benefits immeasurably from their tireless work to understand and shape the debate in America.

In the summer of 2007, I participated in a Presidential Candidate Forum as part of the Yearly Kos Convention. More than any single event, Yearly Kos convinced me that engaged citizens can rebuild the political debate in positive terms. I am grateful to Gina Cooper, Joan McCarter, Ari Melber, Matt Bai, and the entire Yearly Kos (now Netroots Nation) team for helping to restore my faith in civic debate.

"Writing a book," George Orwell famously noted, is "like a long bout with some painful illness." In my bout, I was lucky to have two people in particular in my corner. My sister is an invaluable sounding board, critic, and friend. I am grateful for her constant feedback that helped to sharpen my thoughts at key stages of the manuscript. And without my wife, Debora, neither my writing, nor anything else I attempt would make it very far. Her patience and non-judgmental advice helped me turn a rickety pile of thoughts into a book that could stand on its own. Along the way, she was rewarded by short deadlines, late nights, and a house that was all too often empty. I am grateful to her more than I can express in words. Without her, this book would simply not exist.

CONTENTS

OUTRIGHT
BARBAROUS

PREFACE

$\mathbf{M}$y decision to write a book on the right-wing punditry's use of violent language came in the days following the horrific massacre of students in Blacksburg, Virginia on April 16, 2007. I had lived for almost a decade in Charlottesville, where I earned my Ph.D. in Cultural Anthropology, so I knew many people connected with Virginia Tech, and spent most of that day on the phone trying to make sure that everyone I knew was alright. Not since September 11 had I felt such a loss of control.

Thankfully, everyone I knew was unharmed, although the same could not be said for the dozens of people whose lives were ended senselessly by the bullets of Seung-Hui Cho. By coincidence, the National Rifle Association (NRA) had held its annual meeting in St. Louis just a few days before the Virginia Tech shootings. In preparation for the meeting, NRA President Wayne LaPierre had circulated a letter to the group's membership, a copy of which was still on the NRA's website as news of the wounded and killed in Virginia appeared in the national media:

> Today is one of the most important days of the year for gun owners. The start of the NRA Annual Meetings is both a

celebration of freedom and a rally for the Second Amendment, but it's also a show of force by gun owners to the enemies of freedom everywhere…They're not interested in lobbying Congress or state legislators. Instead, they want to go global, with the help of anti-gun politicians in countries without the Second Amendment. That arms trade treaty, if ratified by Congress or signed by a future president, would mean a global war on your guns the likes of which has never been seen. But when we gather in St. Louis, we show them we won't be pushed around.[1]

After reading the letter, I sat silently at my desk for a long while. Current events can often turn what would otherwise be ordinary words into statements of significance far beyond their original intent. This was one of those occasions. LaPierre was the most prominent right-wing pundit on gun ownership, author of several books, and a regular on TV talk shows. While he mourned the tragic loss of life in Blacksburg as deeply as every other American, just days prior he had rallied his membership with violent rhetoric. As the most visible advocate for gun safety, the NRA should have known to replace that letter with something more appropriate. Yet, LaPierre's letter was not just about guns or constitutional rights or government policy. It was an effort by a right-wing pundit and political leader to define his opponents through a logic of violence. As such, the decades long political debate to understand the U.S. Constitution as it relates to private ownership of firearms was, according to LaPierre, reduced to war. Those who disagreed with the NRA's views were no longer fellow Americans engaged in civic debate, but rather "enemies" waging a "global war" on guns. In LaPierre's words, those who opposed the NRA blurred together with "enemies" in other "global wars," a phrase eerily similar to the ubiquitous "global war on terror."

I printed out LaPierre's letter and called a friend to meet for coffee to discuss it. "My goodness," I said. "This letter talks about you, me and most people I know in the same language the media uses to talk about terrorists." Suddenly, LaPierre's political opponents were traitors to America. To make matters worse, other right-wing pundits amplified the NRA's violent language in the broadcast media. On April 17, Bill O'Reilly accused "the far left" of waiting only "minutes" before using the mass murder to advance an "anti-gun story."[2] The following day, columnist Ann Coulter argued that strict gun laws, state legislators, and administrators were the real cause behind the deaths in Blacksburg, not the gunman:

> Virginia Tech spokesman Larry Hincker praised the legislature for allowing the school to disarm lawful gun owners on the faculty and student body, thereby surrendering every college campus in the state to deranged mass murderers.[3]

The effort to frame the Blacksburg massacre as the product of left-wing politics echoed from coast to coast. The end result, as *Washington Post* columnist E. J. Dionne observed, was not merely offensive, but fundamentally damaging to the American tradition of getting things done.[4] Innocent people died on the Virginia Tech campus, but what suffered from the right-wing media tactics that followed was American pragmatism. Dionne was correct in every aspect of his argument except one: pragmatism had suffered in more than just the gun control debate. Pragmatic solutions to every major political issue collapsed during the years of the Bush administration, under the strain of violent language heaped on our national debate by right-wing pundits.

This was a watershed moment for me in terms of how I saw the right-wing media, and by extension political debate in America at large. Beyond my personal reactions, however, the violent language from LaPierre opened my eyes and ears to something much larger than just the rhetoric of the gun debate. The more I looked around, the more I noticed that violent language was everywhere in American politics. Just about every policy issue being debated had been swept up in words that evoked violent imagery, metaphor and logic. Americans left and right seemed to be thinking about every social problem, security challenge, and economic goal in violent terms. Yet, the loudest and most consistent voices in this trend in violent language were right-wing pundits—the Republican-leaning political talkers whose voices and faces appear constantly on TV and in the pages of best-selling books.

At the time of the Virginia Tech shootings, I was just beginning a speaking tour for my first book, *Framing The Debate*, in which I examined the rhetorical strategies that U.S. presidents have used throughout history to relay big ideas to the public. The experience of researching and writing *Framing the Debate* had grounded me in this country's heritage of great rhetoric, and had helped me develop my own approach to political debate using the tools of frame analysis. With these tools in mind, the problem I witnessed unfold in the media after the Blacksburg tragedy came into focus. A "violent frame" had taken hold of America's broadcast political media as seen through the writing and speech of a core group of pundits, and that violent frame now undermined the productive flow of ideas and solutions in American civic life.

Curiously, the right-wing has not always been the source of violent rhetoric in American political debate. A key figure on the left, Franklin D. Roosevelt, made early use of a violent frame to rally the American public behind government efforts to end poverty, likening the fight against joblessness to an "emergency of war."[5] Lyndon Johnson subsequently promoted the "War on Poverty" as a series of policies in his 1964 State of the Union Address, using the "war" frame to explain how he planned to restore economic justice in America:

> This administration today, here and now, declares unconditional war on poverty in America. I urge this Congress and all Americans to join with me in that effort. It will not be

a short or easy struggle, no single weapon or strategy will suffice, but we shall not rest until that war is won. The richest Nation on earth can afford to win it. We cannot afford to lose it...For the war against poverty will not be won here in Washington. It must be won in the field, in every private home, in every public office, from the courthouse to the White House.[6]

More recently, in his 2007 acceptance speech before the Nobel Prize committee, Al Gore also invoked a war frame, likening the challenge of lowering carbon dioxide levels in the Earth's atmosphere to mobilizing a nation for military action.[7] While an implicitly violent concept in the broadest sense, Roosevelt, Johnson and Gore used the "war" metaphor as a way to redefine public participation in programs aimed at ending social inequalities and global problems. Shamefully, Johnson also tried to use violent rhetoric to defeat his political opponent in the presidential election of 1964 in the infamous "Daisy" ad, which cut from a shot of a little girl counting flower petals to an exploding atomic bomb to imply that a vote for the Republican candidate Barry Goldwater would bring nuclear war upon America. Johnson was severely rebuked on both sides of the political spectrum for the use of violence, and the ad was pulled.

Outright Barbarous focuses primarily on the period after 9/11, shedding light on the multitude of ways right-wing pundits turned violent rhetoric into a dominant idiom for talking politics. While each of the writers and broadcasters examined had risen to prominence long before 2001, some even using violent rhetoric in the earlier phases of their work, their proclivity to speak and write in violent terms increased dramatically after the attacks of 9/11—reaching a crescendo in the period leading up to the 2006 elections. The end result was a crippling of any recognizably productive discussion of the issues facing the American public, having been replaced by continuing attempts to define politics as a "war" and political opponents as dangerous enemies. Al Gore described this process poignantly as the loss of "reason" in American civic discourse, meaning that the rhetoric of right-wing pundits created such a poisoned national debate than any public talk of solving problems and building the future—whether initiated from the political right or left—couldn't survive.[8] Today, with the 2008 presidential election season underway, the same pattern has repeated itself and shows no signs of slowing down.

Given this situation, what, then, is the solution? Once we get a glimpse of how widespread violent language has become in the media, what can we do about it? First and foremost, it is crucial to recognize that American culture and legal tradition warns us wisely of the grave danger inherent in trying to limit political speech. Clamping down on freedom of expression in reaction to violent language is not only wrong, it is counterproductive to democracy. To step back and take a closer look at the prominent voices driving violent language in the media, however, has nothing to do with limiting freedom of speech, but is a normal, healthy part of civic life, albeit a part that we have overlooked in recent years. Hence, the first step must be to do what so rarely gets done in an age of 24-hour news media: to take a longer, more detailed look at what right-wing pundits have said with the goal of understanding the kind of public conversation their words have built. At the end of the day, American tradition teaches us to move forward not by telling people what they can and cannot say—how they can or cannot express themselves—but by building a better discussion.

By pausing to read what is actually being said, we can take stock of the violent language coursing through our political system, put it aside, and begin again. This kind of reflective analysis transcends any given political moment, but it is particularly germane today. At the end of two presidential terms dominated by the violent policies of the Bush-Cheney administration, more and more Americans feel the time has come to reflect on how violence impacts our core political issues. Moreover, while the violence in our political debate did not begin after the attacks of September 11, 2001, those events were followed by a noticeable increase in violent speech from right-wing pundits. That American political rhetoric has become more violent following 9/11 renders the tragedy that much more troubling. Freeing ourselves fully from the fear that still lingers as a result of that day will require not only effective national security and foreign policy, but a rejection of the violent frame of political debate—a frame forced onto the world stage via horrific actions and words. In refusing to accept violent rhetoric, we open our minds to consider what political debate might be like without it. The result is a rediscovery of the tireless drive to identify the core challenges of our time, and then to do what needs to be done to achieve a meaningful, enduring future.

Jeffrey Feldman
New York City
January 2008

1. VIOLENT RIGHT

Most people who bother with the matter at all would admit that the English language is in a bad way, but it is generally assumed that we cannot by conscious action do anything about it.[1]

In his essay "Politics and the English Language," written over fifty years ago, George Orwell raised a question fitting for Americans today. Lamenting the incessant vagueness of political speech and writing in England, Orwell surmised that the situation resulted from the need of politicians to muddy the waters on a host of topics that nobody could simply stand up and state clearly to the public without triggering widespread horror. In Orwell's time, these topics were colonial domination and totalitarian rule. "Sheer cloudy vagueness," as Orwell saw it, became the politician's method for "defending the indefensible." In the mouths of politicians, Orwell surmised, the English language had taken on a "decadence" calculated to numb the listener. Words no longer relayed meaning or clear thought or direct solutions, but instead fell upon the facts "like soft snow."[2] He warned that the overly ornate, bureaucratic language of politicians had become a problem for English democracy, urging the general public to be on guard against "ready-made phrases" in political speech that could easily "anaesthetize" a portion of their brains.[3] As a solution, Orwell offered six rules that he believed could regenerate even the most vague and problematic political language:

Never use a metaphor, simile or other figure of speech which you are used to seeing in print.

Never use a long word where a short will do.

If it is possible to cut a word out, always cut it out.

Never use the passive where you can use the active.

Never use a foreign phrase, a scientific word or a jargon word if you can think of an everyday English equivalent.

Break any of these rules sooner than say anything outright barbarous.[4]

As I read Orwell's essay, I was struck by how aptly it described contemporary American politics. The "outright barbarous" speech that clouds politics today, however, is no longer an ornate bureaucratic dialect, but the violent rhetoric of right-wing pundits.

Violent language poisons American politics more and more each day, rendering our civic debate muddy and vague. With books that fill our bookstores, and chat shows that saturate our broadcast airwaves, a cohort of right-wing pundits now dominates our civic life with a brand of speech that fills everyone with worry and fear, but leaves our politics virtually devoid of real solutions to real problems. Instead of hopeful, optimistic pragmatism focused on achieving a shared future full of promise, our political debates are neck-deep in the pessimism and uncertainty that flows from violent rhetoric. The result is a frustration felt in every corner of America's ongoing political conversation. Once healthy discussion of the relationship between religion and democracy is now dominated by a militant call to arms in a so-called "war on Christmas." An elaborate, but necessary debate about trade, wages and immigration has been replaced by shrill cries about alien "conquest" and the "death" of civilization. And most alarmingly, once spirited conversation about elections have been overwhelmed by cries of "civil war" accusing liberals of plotting in concert with terrorists to undermine, weaken and destroy America. And yet, while most Americans are concerned by politics dominated by violent rhetoric from the right, we all too quickly assume, as Orwell remarked, "that we cannot by conscious action do anything about it."

In fact, every American can do something about the violent language that poisons our political debate. We can refuse to accept it, talk about the important issues it obscures, and work together to improve our civic discourse. In this book, I follow that exact prescription by analyzing the violent words of a core group of influential right-wing pundits, all of whom have achieved extraordinary prominence in print and broadcast media. Hardly a day goes by without their words filling our newspapers, magazines, and airwaves. As a result of this small but powerful cadre, our political debate is in crisis, though, unfortunately, most Americans do not know the work of these right-wing pundits well enough to see exactly how they weigh down politics with violent language.

In the chapters that follow, I examine not just the ideas of these pundits, but the words in their books and the transcripts of their television appearances. My strategy is to read their words in order to tease out the thread of violence they have stitched into the public debate. In each case, the pundits whose words I examine lean right politically and dominate the political debate on a range of the most contested political issues of our time, from guns, family, and religion to immigration, diversity, security, and media. After examining the words and ideas of these pundits, I then suggest practical steps that can be taken to restart the discussion on each of the topics trapped by violent rhetoric. These steps are intended to revive an optimistic, deliberative debate in American politics and to focus the discussion on real solutions to the challenges we face as a nation.

Why take on the issue of violent language in political debate now, given the problems that America faces in the world, from Iraq, to the climate crisis, healthcare, the weak dollar and so many more?

Because our collective ability to meet the challenges of our day depends on our dedication and willingness to maintain a functioning, viable, and productive democracy. Violent language weakens the balance of power that sustains our American form of government; it is a toxin in the system, an element that impedes key functions and shuts down one part of the body after another until, eventually, the system collapses. Left untreated, violent language bleeds into a general violent outlook for all issues, no matter how large or small. At first, only foreigners, rogue nations, and political opponents are seen as threats. When the system collapses, however, we see threats in every neighbor, every coworker, and in every family member.

The emergence of right-wing pundits who use violent logic, language and arguments in national political debate did not gradually take shape over a long stretch of time, but rose up at a starling speed in the lead-up to the national elections of 2004 and 2006. As the horrific extent of the Iraqi military occupation waxed and George W. Bush's popularity waned, a hitherto sarcastic right-wing punditry seemed all at once to step into a new rhetorical frame. Suddenly, with Bush's re-election in doubt, casualties spiraling out of control, and revelations of U.S. military human rights abuses popping up all over, right-wing pundits shifted their tone from critique to conspiracy. The shift is summed up best by the opening line in Dinesh D'Souza's book *The Enemy at Home*: "The cultural left in this country is responsible for causing 9/11." As if that is not enough, D'Souza's book also accuses liberals of engaging in civil war with the rest of America and of harboring a violent dream that complements the terrorist goals of Osama Bin Laden, yearns for the destruction of U.S. military forces in Iraq, and seeks the downfall of the United States. D'Souza's book filled mainstream bookstores, giving scholarly legitimacy to violent accusations of high treason against vast segments of the American populace.

Violent language as a manner of speech amongst right-wing

pundits reached a crescendo in the days leading up to the 2006 mid-term elections. Ann Coulter joked about "nuking" Iran; Bill O'Reilly talked about the "war on Christmas;" Pat Buchanan and Lou Dobbs spoke of the "invasion" and "conquest" of America by immigrants. I even came across a discussion of the "war against the war," in which an anti-war protest was discussed as if it was a war. Every political topic seemed clouded over by a right-wing pundit using violence language.

In the months following the 2006 mid-term elections, I penned several blog posts questioning whether the rise of violent rhetoric on the right might be a dangerous development that could possibly transform, through a sudden incident, into actual physical violence. Turning to the work of Hannah Arendt, in particular her masterful study of politics and violence, *On Violence*, I began to realize that the last significant violent turn in American political ideology and practice involved both the political right and the left.[5] The late 1960s was a time, Arendt explained, where people increasingly believed that violence could actually produce controlled political outcomes. The result was an era in U.S. politics where a broad range of different political organizations and movements each took up violence, a product of the widespread acceptance of Mao Tse-tung's aphorism, "political power grows at the barrel of a gun."[6] Arendt watched this moment lead to assassinations and mass chaos in urban centers, and thus argued that violence was problematic because it led to outcomes in politics that could not be controlled. Violence, she explained, drawing on a famous quote from Karl Marx , may be the birth pang of a new political body, but we would never say that labor pains were the cause of a birth. The same is true with violence, which occasionally happens at times of great political change, but is not the cause of such change.

Arendt's thoughts on violence helped me to clarify several aspects of the trend in right-wing violent language that I was tracking in the media. First, I realized that the use of violent language was not accidental, but was the product of a shift in the political philosophy on which the right-wing punditry built their ideas. The shift was from a rhetoric of parody and burlesque to one of violence and accusation. Second, Arendt helped me to clarify exactly what role violence was playing in the worldview of the right-wing punditry. Most right-wing pundits see the power of the state as residing ultimately in the monopoly over violence, an idea that comes from the writings of the German philosopher Max Weber.[7] This, however, is not the political philosophy that guided the framers of the U.S. Constitution. In other words, violent rhetoric is not just a question of linguistic style, but a sign that a political philosophy in conflict with American deliberative democracy has captured the imagination of many right-wing pundits. Several factors have led to the emergence of violence among right-wing pundits, but the events of 9/11 seem central. In the wake of the attacks, right-wing pundits grew ever more convinced that the continued survival of the United States depended on its willingness to use violence. The more violent language filled the airwaves of America's broadcast media, the more this new and disturbing logic of violence and power seemed to saturate public thinking.

Lastly, Arendt helped me to see that American deliberative democracy was a form of government crafted as a replacement for earlier forms of rule by violence. In a discussion of American politics, the opposite of violence has never been non-violence, but participation—specifically, participation in deliberative democracy. The quintessential American town hall meetings that Jefferson imagined happening amongst small, mostly agricultural communities in rural colonial America were not just a system for accomplishing the needs of the people, but a bulwark against tyrannical rule that resulted from a royal monopoly on all forms of power.

After considering the violent language of right-wing pundits, I began to see the language of America's elected leaders in a new light, particularly the rhetoric of President Bush and Vice President Cheney. From the start of its term in office, the Bush administration has been unrivaled in its ability to manipulate the public via the media. As such, strong political ties to privately owned, right-wing broadcast media has been its biggest political asset. Yet, beyond their ability to wield control of the means of communication in our country, President Bush and Vice President Cheney embraced violence as a structuring concept in their political speech.

President Bush first stepped in the direction of violent language in the week following the attacks of September 11, when he gave a series of public statements during visits to the White House by foreign dignitaries and U.S. government employees. The stated theme of that week was the mounting of a campaign to fight terrorism on a global scale, but the agenda had much more to do with constructing a new persona for Bush through a series of violent statements threatening the perpetrators of the attacks of 9/11. Over and over again that week, Bush said "we're going to smoke them out of their holes," talking about the impending operations to find the terrorists responsible for 9/11 as if he were a cowboy setting out to kill prairie animals. Attempting much more than a bad John Wayne impersonation in those speeches, Bush was boldly stepping across a line that most presidents rarely crossed: direct calls for the death of other human beings.

That was a week of unimaginable emotional anguish for most Americans, and Bush's foray into violent language was largely hailed as welcome bravado in response to an act of war. While researching my book on presidential speeches in the summer of 2006, I went back to the transcripts of Bush's post-9/11 appearances and found several moments filled with glib references to death and killing. Speaking to employees at the Pentagon on September 17, 2001, for example, Bush said the following in response to a reporter's question:

> I know that this is a different type of enemy than we're used to. It's an enemy that likes to hide and burrow in, and their network is extensive. There are no rules. It's barbaric behavior. They slit throats of women on airplanes in order to achieve an objective that is beyond comprehension. And

they like to hit, and then they like to hide out. But we're going to smoke them out. And we're adjusting our thinking to the new type of enemy.[8]

A sitting U.S. president using his own voice to advocate graphic violence signaled a disturbing change in our political system. Events can be relayed in a variety of ways. President Bush chose violent descriptions to sum up the problem. At first glance, one would assume that his words had the obvious impact of injecting fear into American consciousness. Indeed, they did. In the months that followed September 11, 2001, the country grew more and more afraid of knife-yielding terrorists on planes and more afraid of hidden threats, as waves of panic spread back and forth across the country. President Bush's metaphoric description of terrorists as animals skilled at hiding and committing barbaric acts of murder led people to accept that safety and security could only be restored by an equally violent process of hunting and killing. The violence of 9/11 had made Americans nervous about danger from the skies. As President Bush began to describe hidden threats of "barbaric" violence, Americans began to worry about which dangerous persons might be hiding in their own communities, or standing behind them in the line at the grocery store, or sitting one seat over on the subway.

President Bush's turn to violent language was foreshadowed by his prior interest in the bellicose foreign policy vision of right-wing think tanks that had been pushing violent foreign policy since the late 1990s, such as the Project For The New American Century.[9] His speeches also served as a green light to right-wing pundits, inviting them to step into a violent political idiom. Perhaps nobody embodied this more than Ann Coulter. Having made a name for herself as a pundit willing to talk about sex, Coulter's first column after 9/11 called for Americans to "invade" Muslim nations, "kill" their leaders and "convert" foreign citizens to Christianity. Coulter had lost a close friend in one of the planes that crashed on 9/11. Angry rhetoric in response to personal loss was a form of expression that most Americans understood, even as they felt uncomfortable with it. Nonetheless, Coulter's violent language took mainstream American media to a place it had not been since at least the 1950s, if not the 1930s. Another important step was about to be taken, however, and in this case it would be prominent pundits in the media who took the lead. Whereas Bush had turned to violent language as a technique for dehumanizing the enemy—talking about terrorists as if they were animals to be hunted and exterminated—right-wing pundits on radio, television and in print slowly infused violent language into domestic political debate. Radicalized right-wing activists calling Democrats "murderers" had been a familiar, albeit disturbing, aspect of the abortion right's debate. What changed, however, was the sudden linking of violent death in 9/11 to issues that had hitherto been discussed solely in terms of competing social agendas.

Speaking in the days after the events of 9/11 on *The 700 Club*, Pat Robertson and Jerry Falwell blamed the death and destruction on liberal groups in America:

> FALWELL: The ACLU's got to take a lot of blame for this.
> ROBERTSON: Well, yes.
> FALWELL: And, I know that I'll hear from them for this. But, throwing God out successfully with the help of the federal court system, throwing God out of the public square, out of the schools. The abortionists have got to bear some burden for this because God will not be mocked. And when we destroy 40 million little innocent babies, we make God mad. I really believe that the pagans, and the abortionists, and the feminists, and the gays and the lesbians who are actively trying to make that an alternative lifestyle, the ACLU, People For the American Way, all of them who have tried to secularize America. I point the finger in their face and say 'you helped this happen'.
> ROBERTSON: Well, I totally concur, and the problem is

we have adopted that agenda at the highest levels of our government. And so we're responsible as a free society for what the top people do. And, the top people, of course, is the court system.[10]

Falwell's idea that "we make God mad so God uses terrorists to exact revenge" found its correlate in equally shocking attempts by left-wing pundits and intellectuals to somehow blame the murders of 9/11 on social and economic conservatives. Political activist and professor Ward Churchill, for example, claimed infamously that the victims of the attacks were somehow responsible for their own deaths by virtue of their employment in a capitalist society, and was deservedly excoriated for doing so. Nonetheless, the limited amount of violent rhetoric from the left that followed 9/11 quickly dissipated. Falwell's and Robertson's exchange, by contrast, nudged open a door that more and more pundits in the right-wing media began to walk through because of two additional factors that had set up a tectonic shift in right-wing rhetoric.

The first factor was that Falwell's and Robertson's comments occurred in a post-2000 America where key evangelical leaders wield unprecedented national influence. Most notable among these evangelical leaders is James Dobson, founder and Chairmen of the Christian parenting organization Focus on the Family, and a best-selling right-wing author who writes and speaks about the importance of using physical violence as a technique for disciplining children. Dobson played a prominent role in turning out the vote in the 2000 presidential election, and as a result, his authoritarian ideas on parenting are now widely discussed in the mainstream media. In the period immediately after 9/11, however, the influence of Dobson went far beyond the question of raising children to the much broader issue of how the terrain of political debate in America had shifted in the months prior to the attacks. The Dobson era in the Republican Party heralded a newfound comfort with the use of violent terms on a host of social issues, including homosexuality, the family, and education.

The second factor was the resurgence of the National Rifle Association as a political force in right-wing politics. Then NRA Vice President Wayne LaPierre had already employed violent language to argue against gun control laws in the year prior to September 11. In mid-2000, for example, LaPierre accused Bill Clinton of having blood on his hands for not enforcing gun laws, pushing the argument that Democrats allowed violent crime to happen in order advance a liberal agenda to deny gun owners their constitutional rights. LaPierre's rhetoric was so inflammatory that then NRA President Charlton Heston felt the need to redress him.[11] Nonetheless, with the election of George W. Bush, LaPierre emerged as the premier author and TV pundit on gun issues. The dual rise of authoritarian Evangelicals and NRA leadership in the Republican Party and the media prepared American civic debate to acquiesce to a higher level of violent rhetoric.

The run up to the 2004 presidential election further increased the volume and frequency of violent rhetoric in the right-wing media—a key transformation in the Republican Party that became embodied in the words and persona of Dick Cheney. Caught in a cycle of bad news from Iraq, human rights abuses, tales of secret prisons, and mounting corruption scandals, the Republican Party launched a PR campaign to equate a Democratic return to the White House with increased terrorist attacks. Speaking to a packed crowd in Des Moines, Iowa on September 9, 2004, Cheney brought violence to the heart of his campaign rhetoric:

> It's absolutely essential that eight weeks from today, on November 2nd, we make the right choice. Because if we make the wrong choice, then the danger is that we'll get hit again, that we'll be hit in a way that will be devastating from the standpoint of the United States, and that we'll fall back into the pre-9/11 mind set if you will, that in fact these terrorist attacks are just criminal acts, and that we're not really at

war. I think that would be a terrible mistake for us. We have to understand it is a war.[12]

Rather than tone down his speeches in response to criticism, Cheney steeled his resolve and rallied the party faithful. By 2006, arguing that electoral victory for the Democrats would lead to the mass death of Americans by terrorists had became the core election strategy of the Republican Party. As election day neared, then Republican National Committee chairman Ken Mehlman commissioned a political ad called "The Stakes," combining a ticking-bomb soundtrack, images of Osama Bin Laden, video clips from terrorist training films, and shots of exploding nuclear bombs. The violent message of the ad was that a vote for the Democrats was a vote for mass annihilation at the hands of nuclear-armed al Qaeda terrorists. The arc that had begun with President Bush using violence to dehumanize terrorists was now complete.

At this point in the discussion, many people often mistake a concern for violent rhetoric with attempts to censor political speech or limit freedom of expression. It is an understandable reaction brought on by the deep affection Americans hold for the First Amendment of the U.S. Constitution. Freedom of speech—no matter how obscene, offensive or threatening that speech may be—cannot be limited, curtailed or regulated without violating civil rights, or so the argument goes.

In general, the American system recognizes that speech is not to be limited up to the point that it presents "a clear and present danger of action of the kind the State is empowered to prevent and punish."[13] Shouting "Fire!" in a crowded theater, which we are not free to do, is the classic example. If we walk into a theater and cause mass hysteria by yelling "Fire!" without due cause, there will be a penalty for our destructive action. If someone says to a friend "Shoot that man there," and he does so—that speech is part of the crime and, thus falls under the criminal statutes against murder. Moreover, what we all too often forget in our rush to assert freedom of expression is the other side of the First Amendment, a side that is in many ways even more important: freedom from compulsion. Compelling individuals to speak or express themselves in a specific way, particularly by the state, damages the First Amendment as much if not more than limiting individual expression. If, for example, a newspaper editor were compelled to print the news each morning according to the dictates of the White House Communications Director, that compulsion would infringe upon the First Amendment rights of far more people than just the editor. Anyone who read or heard about the information in that paper—as government had compelled the editor to include it—would be deprived of his or her First Amendment rights. Moreover, when it comes to violence in speech, context is everything. Violent language appears in the Bible, in Homer's works, and in fairy tales, for example, but our system would never tolerate laws limiting the circulation or reading of *The Book of Job*, *The Iliad* or *Little Red Riding Hood*.

Following these basic principles, the U.S. federal government and court system have treated broadcast media, with its unrivalled ability to penetrate every aspect of American life, as a medium with potential for endangering certain individuals if left completely unregulated. In 2007, for example, the Federal Communications Commission issued a report studying the effects of violent television on America's children. The FCC came to the conclusion that efforts should be made to "channel" violent programming into those times of the day when children were least likely to be exposed to it and, wherever possible, to notify viewers in advance of violent content through a ratings system.[14] Most of us benefit from this two-pronged approach without even thinking about it. When it is time for certain entertainment shows to start, a viewer discretion warning appears to alert us to any violent content or language, and in that moment we decide whether to continue watching or to choose another program. Most importantly, if we have children, that warning gives us a chance to decide if the content of the show is appropriate for them.

As much as our system cares about protecting children from unwittingly coming into content with violent language in entertainment, it bends over backwards to make sure that none of the same measures infringe upon political speech. When it comes to political speech, the concern over compulsion is so deeply rooted in our culture that most scheduling restrictions or viewer advisories are held at bay. The exception to that rule are political shows that step clearly into a potential danger zone by virtue of their use of adult language. The best example of a political show that has been time channeled and includes viewer advisories is *Real Time with Bill Maher*. Clearly, there are commercial disadvantages to airing a political talk show after 11:00pm, but they are balanced by the benefits of helping parents protect their children. That is not to say that Bill Maher's language is "bad" for children, but only that the content of the discussions he leads are widely viewed as inappropriate for audiences under a certain age. Viewer advisories and time channeling are widely seen as helpful precisely because it is so difficult to define "violence" in such a way that would allow producers of content to predictably comply with regulations limiting it.

While not a source of violent rhetoric, Bill Maher's show includes many adult themes. As such, it points to a question about political media rarely asked in discussions of regulatory efforts with respect to violent language in broadcast TV: Are most political talk shows news or entertainment? Maher's show, with its signature combination of comedy monologue and celebrity roundtable discussion, is clearly a form of entertainment designed to challenge viewers to think critically about politics. Its content is political, but *Real Time* is entertainment. For many other political talk shows on TV, particularly those on FOX News, the line between news and entertainment becomes blurry if not invisible altogether. For example, on an April 2007 episode of *The O'Reilly Factor*, host Bill O'Reilly and his guest Geraldo Rivera discussed the issue of drunk driving, crime and illegal immigration through an exchange of violent rhetoric that many believed was unprecedented for a "news" broadcast. Given how disconcerted so many viewers were in response to this particular episode of O'Reilly's show, it suggests that the type of violent exchange it featured warranted the viewer discretion advisory and time channeling required of a show more explicitly presented as entertainment. The question, in other words, is not one of censorship, but of the best way to protect viewers given the unprecedented power of broadcast media in our society and the number of political talk shows that inhabit the gray zone between news and entertainment.

Like most books that attempt to describe a broad issue in political speech, this book is by necessity incomplete. There are pundits whose writing or speech is more violent than those discussed in the pages that follow, but who were excluded either because they had little if any presence in broadcast media, had not published a widely read book, or were not recognized as top pundits on a given political issue. As a result, all of the pundits included in this book are at the height of their careers, are highly successful both in monetary and political terms, and have ample public records of their speech. My analysis focuses on right-wing pundits because the problem of violent language is anchored on that side of what has become a highly polarized media industry.

While each chapter stands on its own, the entire book presents a cross section of the core issues that dominate political debate in America: guns, immigration, liberalism, culture, religion, families, and terrorism. No list of issues can exhaust all potential avenues for analysis, and that is not the intention within these chapters. By reading the range of issues dominated by violent language as presented in this book, readers will inevitably begin to examine the issues that are most present in their own lives. In other words, I accept as given that no reader will resist the temptation to compare their own analysis to mine as they read. How does violent language influence the abortion debate? The debate over presidential powers?

The environment? Healthcare? The level to which violent language has already saturated our national debate means that pragmatic and productive discussions of most issues in American political life have now suffered the effects.

Every pundit scrutinized in the chapters of this book will likely continue to be an influential force in American politics for some time to come. Writers and speakers who continue to use violence to communicate their politics will not only cause widespread alarm, but cloud what little clarity remains in American political debate. Yet, new voices are always emerging. In addition to encouraging people to use each chapter as starting point for their own critical analysis of the political issues that concern them, *Outright Barbarous* also calls for renewed interest in Orwell's six rules of political language. The spirit of progressive pragmatism has periodically stumbled and fallen over the course of American history, but it never stays down long. As such, this book, while shedding a light on those who feed violent language into the political discussion, ultimately invites readers to dedicate themselves to rebuilding a healthy national debate in America.

2. THE WAR ON GUNS

On February 1, 2002, Wayne LaPierre, Executive Vice President of the National Rifle Association, addressed a packed crowd at the Conservative Political Action Conference (CPAC). The title of his speech was "Frightened, or Free?" and from the very first word it was destined to be a classic of right-wing violent rhetoric. The subject of the speech was not so much gun ownership, but the violent abuses that Americans had to endure in airport security in the wake of September 11, 2001. These abuses were contrasted with what LaPierre saw as an unacceptable level of concern for the rights and well-being of the most violent mass murderers in history—radical Islamic terrorists. The heart of LaPierre's speech was his description of the kind of techniques foisted on Americans in airports:

> You see women cringe as security men let their wands linger between their legs. You see countless innocent American citizens—even pilots themselves—dumping out pockets and purses, turning over nail files, tweezers, pen knives and key chains, and then subjected to humiliating physical indignities that grow more sordid with each day they're tolerated. Congressman John Dingell, who has a

steel hip joint and surgically-implanted ankle pins, was asked to drop his pants at Washington's Reagan National Airport....For what, are we sacrificing all reason and judgment? No one is any safer and we know it. But everyone is delayed, defiled and demeaned. And when it doesn't work, where will it stop? When we're all naked? Boarding planes in airline-issued hospital smocks? I guess it's okay to wand-rape someone's daughter in public, but no profiling! No, we don't want to risk offending an Islamic ex-con with two aliases and no job, paying cash for a one-way airline ticket with no luggage, whose shoes are packed with plastic explosives. Who're we fooling? Terrorists fit into fairly narrow categories of gender, age, nationality and religion.[1]

While many Americans may not be acquainted with the term "wand-rape," LaPierre's description was familiar far beyond the confines of the CPAC audience. The less-than secure feeling most people get when passing through airport security had already become a point of contention, frustration and ridicule by early 2002. What many people may not intuit, however, is the degree to which LaPierre saw the new inconveniences not just as annoying or physically invasive, but as a systematic effort by the United States government to defraud citizens of their freedoms. The irony, of course, was that LaPierre—who is still one of the most high-profile right-wing pundits in the country—was making an argument that put him at odds with other right-wing authoritarians and on a similar page as some liberals. This irony was illustrated shortly after LaPierre's CPAC speech when he appeared on FOX's *Hannity & Colmes* to discuss his "wand-rape" remark. On most shows, viewers would expect LaPierre and Hannity to be in agreement and Colmes to be the odd man out, but this time, the opposite was true:

COLMES: Wayne, it's Alan. I never thought the day would come when you and I would be on the same page, after all the times you've come on this program and we've done battle about guns, but I think you have a great point. Indeed, your statement that freedom is the first bargaining chip of a scared people is reminiscent of what was said by Benjamin Franklin when he said "They who'd give up essential liberty to obtain a little temporary safety deserve neither liberty nor safety." Your comment's in the same vein, and I wholeheartedly concur with you, sir.[2]

Colmes was careful not to endorse LaPierre's final point about ethnic or racial profiling, but simply to concur that invasive airport searches struck many as a violation of individual freedoms—not because Americans were not willing or interested in security at airports, but because the methods chosen seemed to lack professionalism and common sense.

Revealing far more than just his view of security wands, however, LaPierre's 2002 CPAC speech was a window into the logic of violence that frames his view of government and politics at a level far greater than the issue of gun ownership. In many instances, he brings in the word "freedom" to make his point, but in this case it is a distraction from his main bogeyman: government. [3] LaPierre, like so many conservatives, discusses government as if it were the angry giant in Jack and the Beanstalk with the totalitarian agenda of a Soviet military state. When airport security seemingly neither secured airports nor gave passengers a sense of well-being, LaPierre saw much more than the issue of security and personnel management; he saw an agenda by government to strip citizens of the individual right to use guns to guard against violence. In his vision, violence against citizens is inevitable and the only guarantee of protection from that violence is for citizens to own guns that they can use when threatened.

In 2003, LaPierre published *Guns, Freedom and Terrorism*, a play on the title of his 1995 book *Guns, Crime, and Freedom*. While *Guns, Freedom and Terrorism* is not exclusively about terrorism, LaPierre builds a case that the best security solution to the problem of terrorist attacks is for more private citizens to own and carry guns. Using 9/11 as a departure point as he had in his 2002 CPAC speech, LaPierre argues in the book that a nation's willingness to safeguard the rights of all its citizens to own guns is the key to keeping democracy afloat in a sea of violence. Even more than those arguments, however, LaPierre's strategic use of violent rhetoric creates some of the most entrenched emotional obstacles of any right-wing writer who regularly makes the rounds of TV and radio. At the most fundamental level, LaPierre describes a view of life as a struggle to prepare for inevitable, violent confrontation with other people seeking to do us harm. This struggle unfolds in the context of a government that is completely powerless to protect against such violence, but which is nonetheless marked by an insatiable desire to wield instruments of violence itself. It is a bleak vision of the world where guns are the only truly effective barrier between the individual and certain death by violence. As such, the individual in possession of a gun for the purpose of firing on those who will commit acts of violent crime or terror becomes, in LaPierre's logic, the great symbol of democratic freedom.[4] He describes everyday life in America as if violent tragedy stood waiting outside the doorstep of every home, repeating the word "violence" over and over again to make his point. Complex discussion on security, democracy and freedom are reduced to falsely constructed scenarios where the hero with the gun saves the day—or in most cases, is prevented from doing so by a government that is all-powerful and inevitably tilting towards totalitarianism.

Nowhere is this perspective more apparent than in LaPierre's discussion of "armed pilots." According to LaPierre, most of the tragic events that unfolded on September 11, 2001 could have been prevented if airline pilots had carried loaded pistols for the purposes of shooting anyone who threatened their planes. There is, thus, a "moral imperative" for America to arm its commercial airline pilots. But lest we get confused about exactly what this moral imperative stipulates, LaPierre describes in perfect clarity the "three possible" types of armed pilots. The first kind of armed pilots are terrorists who seize control of airplanes and fly them into buildings. The second kind are soldiers flying military aircraft equipped with weapons for shooting down commercial airplanes that have been hijacked. The latter was already in existence on September 11, 2001, but did not prevent the attacks. This leaves the third and final definition:

> The third definition of "armed pilot" covers the 125,000 highly trained men and women we entrust with our lives on any one of the 20,000 domestic airline flights that criss-cross America every day. It means that these good people are prepared—with training and the proper tools—to defend the controls of their airplanes, thus protecting the lives of their passengers and countless innocents on the ground. Unfortunately, that definition did not exist when Osama Bin Laden's terror cadres boarded four commercial flights on September 11, 2001.[5]

Interestingly, LaPierre does not suggest that pilots be armed with electric stun guns or mace or other innovations designed specifically to deal with potential assaults on an in-flight cockpit or airline passengers. "Armed," in LaPierre's discussion of airline pilots, means only "with handguns." It means nothing else. The resulting scenario escalates the discussion of airline security to a heightened level of panic. The logic that makes this idea work is LaPierre's vision of a world where violent assaults on individuals are inevitable, all laws and institutions are powerless to stop them, and the only guarantee for survival is for citizens to be prepared to fire a gun at the oncoming danger.

There are of course many alternatives to this view of the world, for both pilots and airline security in general. What if, for example, pilots were "armed" with an array of resources for securing the plane that began long before they even entered the plane, such as separating people from all unnecessary baggage prior to getting onboard?

While it is never discussed much, the men who hijacked the planes on September 11, 2001 did so using weapons in their carry-on luggage. Given that reality, the logical choice to prevent such a repeat instance, it would seem, is not placing guns in the hands of pilots to counter knife or gun-wielding hijackers, but to partially ban carry-on luggage. In such a system, passengers could request a permit in advance and pay a fee to carry bags onto the plane, but only upon rigorous inspection, and subject to significantly increased limitations. In fact, part of the problem with airplane security these days is not just that there are more terrorists in the world, but the increasing tendency for passengers to carry as much luggage on board as physically possible. Loading up all the roll-on luggage, shopping bags and guitar cases that contemporary passengers carry on board has become a logistical nightmare all by itself, even before we take into account any threat of terrorism. Most of the congestion experienced in airports post-9/11 results as much from the endless attempts by passengers to carry way too much luggage onto their flights as from the new security threats. In the long run, solving the problem of security on an individual plane may require that we separate people from their luggage in a more systematic and efficient way. Imagine, for example, a system of airline travel that divided people from their luggage even before they arrived at the airport terminal, flew both to the proper destination, and then reunited them in an orderly fashion. To a certain extent, this system is already in place today for everything but carry on luggage, which has become such a large loophole that the 9/11 terrorists were able to exploit it with disastrous results.

My overall point, however, is not to put forward a position paper on airport security, but rather to show that the 9/11 hijackings involved a series of security weaknesses that could have been addressed without the use of guns. By contrast, LaPierre's armed pilots proposal serves only to trap the discussion in the logic of mortal combat, where the only solution is a gun. But why just stop at armed pilots when the 9/11 terrorists posed violent threats to passengers even before they reached their respective flights? That question, while never posed directly by LaPierre in his chapter on armed pilots, is certainly posed in the rest of the book and in most of LaPierre's work. He envisions, after all, an America where citizens are allowed to carry concealed, loaded handguns at all times for purposes of self-defense against the inevitable confrontation with violent crime. What LaPierre suggests is not just arming the people who fly our planes, but a full-scale military escalation of civil society.

Many Americans assume that "gun rights" is the overriding issue advanced by the NRA. However, the key concept that surfaces in *Guns, Freedom, and Terrorism* is the violent anecdote. LaPierre's gifts as both a speaker and writer lay precisely in his ability to use the violent anecdote to drive forward campaigns for the elimination of gun control legislation. LaPierre's accomplishment as a pundit, therefore, is not his contribution to policy debate, but his success at trapping the discussion in a ping-pong match between two bad choices: Either (A) we allow individuals the "right to carry" guns or (B) we allow criminals to make victims of more and more Americans. The false logic that we must choose between "A" or "B" is the problem, but once framed in violent terms, moving to a new level in the debate becomes difficult.

Chapter seven of *Guns, Freedom, and Terrorism*, for example, exemplifies how LaPierre traps the debate by use of the violent anecdote. Titled "The Right To Carry," the chapter begins with stories of heroism and brutal murder where survival is defined in terms of the presence or absence of handguns. In the first instance in Anniston, Alabama, a restaurant patron saves himself and two-dozen other people with his legal, .45-caliber gun. In the second instance in Killeen, Texas, a homicidal maniac kills twenty-two people, none of whom carried guns for self-defense. The contrast is obvious, and yet, the violent anecdote is just the beginning of the discussion. LaPierre quotes Suzanna Gratia Hupp, whose parents were shot to death in Killeen, as a strategy for trapping the debate squarely in the choice between carrying guns and dying a violent death. Transformed by her horrific experience in Killeen into a right to carry activist, Hupp travels the country recounting her tragic story. She ends her speaking engagements, according to LaPierre, by urging her audience to see state law as a force conspiring to prevent them from becoming heroes who will be able to save their loved ones from future tragedy at the hands of violent murderers:

> State law prohibits the concealed carrying of firearms, denying me or someone else the right to have a gun that day to protect ourselves and our loved ones from the rampages of a madman. That's flat-out wrong. And I intend to do everything in my power to change that ill-gotten law to avert needless suffering by others. The violent incidents in Anniston and Killeen ended far differently because of the laws governing the concealed carrying of firearms. Alabama has a fair concealed-carry law, but in Texas the government has said, in effect, that decent citizens can't be trusted to carry firearms for self-protection…Clearly, concealed-carry laws translated to saving the lives of loved ones in a manner similar to health or life insurance. If ever there arises that time when it is needed, no substitute will do, and I don't intend to be victimized again.[6]

The language of murder and victims traps the reader in a debate fenced in by a false choice between carrying a gun and survival itself. Certainly, there are violent crime scenarios where someone uses a concealed gun to fend off an attacker and save a life. Yet, these situations are not only rare, but in many instances, the victim's gun ends up being used against them. None of this concerns LaPierre, however, who pushes the discussion seamlessly from tales of individuals firing on assailants to claims about entire nations reducing violent crime solely as a result of gun possession. The death of Suzanna Gratia Hupp's parents was tragic, but LaPierre does more than just relay the facts. He uses Hupp's narrative as a violent frame advancing a logic wherein gun laws turn citizens into victims, while gun possession turns victims into heroes. The violent anecdote defines the terrain on which subsequent discussion unfolds. Texas, according to LaPierre's logic, was trapped in a state of perpetual victimization because the Democratic governor, Ann Richards, believed that laws and police work prevented violent crime, not citizens carrying concealed weapons. It was not until the state of Texas elected Republican George W. Bush as governor in 1995 that a right-to-carry bill became law.[7]

Moving beyond the tragedy of mass murder in Texas, LaPierre argues that laws blocking the right-to-carry also lead to spikes in crime at the national level. Great Britain, he argues, began passing more stringent gun control laws starting in 1988, while Australia passed comprehensive gun control in 1997. While curbing violence was the promise of English and Australian gun control laws, the end result was actually, LaPierre argues, the loss of liberty and widespread "fraud" by government itself:

> If curbing violence was the promise of "gun control," it has proved to be a cruel lie and a fraud. In both countries, victims of criminal violence are piling up. Ever since gun confiscation orders were instituted, England and Australia have rushed ahead of the rest of the industrialized world in terms of sheer violence by their criminals against the now-disarmed and vulnerable public. In terms of the likelihood of people becoming victims of crime and violence, England and Australia now rank either first or second in the industrialized world, far outstripping the United States in virtually all categories…Violence and shootings—all marked by the mindless brutality of utterly lawless criminals—are controlling and crippling every aspect of modern British society. Yet, self-defense with any of the few firearms allowed for private ownership is a serious crime.[8]

The idea that "every aspect of modern British society" was suddenly crippled by violent crime in the late 1990s is just one example of LaPierre's tendency to exaggerate claims of violence. Strangely, there is a lack of reporting in the global media on how Britain and Australia were crippled without guns, as LaPierre insists. Instead, LaPierre extrapolates bits of data from a Dutch Ministry of Justice Crime Victims Survey, along with details from an article in *The Guardian*, to posit a link between the advent of strict gun control policy and a widespread surge in crime on a national level.

The shootings at Columbine High School on April 20, 1999 ushered LaPierre into the national spotlight in new and disturbing ways. Less than a week after the tragedy, LaPierre was interviewed by Bob Schaeffer and Gloria Burger on *Face the Nation*, where he presented a shaky but calculated effort to reframe the discussion about school children killing each other with guns. Asked by Borger if the killings at Columbine had brought him to support legislation in Congress to hold adults criminally responsible for allowing children access to guns, LaPierre responded:

> LAPIERRE: I--I don't think holding adults criminally responsible unless they're criminally negligent is the answer. And then they should be held accountable. But let me give you four things that would help...
>
> BORGER: Well, would you say—well, you heard what the governor said, that perhaps some of these adults would be held responsible and charged...
>
> LAPIERRE: Well, and that may very well be appropriate in this instance.
>
> BORGER: So—so the question is, how do you keep children from getting access to guns?
>
> LAPIERRE: OK. Let me—let me answer that with these four points, which I think are very important. One, we need

to make our schools safe, and we need to change the way we've been handling things the last two years. We had 6,000 instances the last two years of guns showing up in schools. Do you know how many we prosecuted? I got from the Senate Committee the figures. In '97, five; in '98, eight.
BORGER: Is metal detectors the answer?
LAPIERRE: We—we—we—we have to—we have to do better in terms of prosecution. Every time a child, a student, a juvenile brings a gun to school, we ought to expel him from school and we ought to prosecute the case.[9]

Pivoting away from the legal question of adults giving guns to children, LaPierre focused instead on the lax role of government in prosecuting children who bring guns to school. Hence, LaPierre steals the ball from Borger and turns the issue of kids killed as a result of gun violence into a question of government's failure to enforce the law. He used the same logic eight years later when responding to questions about the 2007 shootings at Virginia Tech, focusing on the Virginia state government's inability to enforce laws barring the mentally ill from purchasing guns, but never arguing that young people should not have guns. In other words, guns are not to blame when students kill students with guns. The blame lies with politicians.

In *Guns, Freedom and Terrorism*, LaPierre makes it clear that his solution to students shooting each other in school is for parents to teach their children responsible gun ownership. The result will be a safer America where parents put guns in the hands of their kids, and kids keep guns away from the classroom. Citing a Rochester, New York "Youth Development Study," LaPierre concludes that children who "received guns from their parents never committed firearm crimes," and children "given guns by a parent were less likely to commit any kind" of crime or use drugs.[10] The logic LaPierre pushes through these statistics is what he calls a "simple truth" about raising children in America:

Raising youngsters who are productive and respectful members of society takes time, requires good parenting, and demands educators who are willing to teach children how to make the best real-life decisions based on fact not on wishful thinking. The fact that the sport-shooting Rochester youths grew up so well was grounded in their parents, who were involved in their lives in many ways; sharing participation in the shooting sports was just one way in which parents chose to make a constructive difference.[11]

LaPierre's claim is not that guns and childhood education should be kept separate, just that guns should not be brought into the physical space of the school building. In fact, his claim is that American children cannot be raised properly unless guns play a key role in their home life and extracurricular activities. The logic that emerges is a concept of education steeped in socialization to the power, responsibility and danger of gun violence. As such, children are either socialized into a world of guns by their parents and teachers at an early age or society risks turning them into ticking time bombs driven by the media to commit violent crimes.[12] LaPierre's lament in response to the massacres at Columbine and Virginia Tech was not just a critique of law enforcement and responsible parenting, but a vision of American education made strong by virtue of a thriving, national gun culture.

The issue pushed out in the national media by the violent language overwhelming the discussion of guns is "justice." The debate is about justice as a system of laws and government in the interest of all citizens, as opposed to justice as the act of an individual vigilante. Hannah Arendt describes American tradition not just as a distinct style of debate, but an alternative understanding of government and power itself:

When the Athenian city-state called its constitution an isonomy, or the Romans spoke of the civitas as their form of government, they had in mind a concept of power and law whose essence did not rely on the command-obedience relationship and which did not identify power and rule or law and command. It was to these examples that the men of the eighteenth-century turned when they ransacked the archives of antiquity and constituted a form of government, a republic, where the rule of law, resting on the power of the people, would put an end to the rule of man over man, which they thought was a "government fit for slaves."[13]

Gun ownership becomes a problem at the point where guns become vehicles for imposing "command-obedience" forms of power on society. This gives meaning to the words of the Second Amendment and direction to a productive debate on guns in America. Arendt's comment dissipates much of the fog imposed on the gun debate by LaPierre's violent framework, where guns are forever trapped within a logic of self-defense and the projection of individual power. Potential for violence, thus, becomes only part of the threat inherent in an oversupply of guns in society. The greater threat is the tendency of guns to catalyze feelings of power and dominance, partly through interaction with the broad effects of so many depictions of guns in the media, but also through the inherent quality of guns themselves.

LaPierre's violent logic is a stark contrast to the America that Arendt describes with such admiration. Whether he is speaking about shootings in schools or writing about parental responsibility to teach children about guns, LaPierre's rhetoric always returns to the image of the individual citizen trying to survive in a world of violence. He may not always come right out and say that our lives are in danger unless the government allows all responsible and law-abiding adults to carry concealed weapons, but his political speech constantly hammers the idea that we are never truly safe unless we place guns as tools of self-defense in the hands of citizens. The discussion that unfolds from LaPierre's rhetoric clouds the actual issue at stake: the principles articulated by the United States Constitution and the kind of society Americans support. LaPierre's violent vision gives shape to a society anchored in vigilantism in and posse comitatus, the practice of using a body of armed men summoned by a sheriff to enforce the law, which was widely prohibited following Reconstruction. In his arguments about violent children and gun crimes, LaPierre is not just calling for a particular interpretation of the Second Amendment, but for the return to a pre-Civil War concept of citizenry and system of law enforcement. Arguing against the personal ownership of guns is the bait that LaPierre dangles in front of those who try to talk their way out of his violent logic. A better alternative is to reframe the entire discussion in terms of upholding Constitutional principle. Effective responses to LaPierre's violent vision, in other words, begin by claiming that faith in the law is the key to civic well-being. Thus, LaPierre's position on "guns" or "gun rights," can be reframed in terms of the danger of a vigilante society. In an America where everyone can be judge and jury simply because they own a gun, vigilantes endanger everyone's safety and security.

With Arendt's observations in mind, the debate Americans should have is not about gun ownership per se, but about the importance of collective institutions to maintain order, safety and justice in society. What can and should make us safe in America? Is it guns or is it the law? In our cleaned up discussion, these questions become helpful, where they once served only to muddy the waters. Gun ownership for sport, for example, poses no threat to the safety and security of society. With the exception of a relatively small number of animal rights activists, there is not a movement to take guns away from hunters. Nor is there a significant number of Americans seeking to ban gun sports, such as target shooting, skeet or biathlon. The issue at stake in these activities is not guns, but the environment and sports. Without well-regulated seasons and responsible hunters, for example, certain populations of wild animals would grow out of control and cause widespread environmental destruction. On the other hand, when people carry concealed weapons or own guns produced for military use, our system of justice is thrown out of balance. Individuals taking up arms does not solve the problem of criminals getting their hands on these weapons and using them to harm others. The solution is better law enforcement, more effective police training, and legislation focused on guns and crime.

Many people tend to get confused on this matter by the speed with which someone like LaPierre uses violent anecdotes to frame his arguments about the Second Amendment, which states: "A well regulated Militia, being necessary to the security of a free State, the right of the people to keep and bear arms, shall not be infringed." But what does that mean? Does it mean, de facto, that Americans have the right to carry a Glock automatic pistol in their purse? Constitutional expert Michael Dorf argues that there are three models for interpreting the Second Amendment, only one of which leads to the idea that Americans have a right to carry:

> The first and second [models] both emphasize the preamble, or "purpose" clause, of the Amendment—the words "a well regulated Militia, being necessary to the security of a free State." The third does not. The first model holds that the right to keep and bear arms belongs to the people collectively rather than to individuals, because the right's only purpose is to enable states to maintain a militia; it is not for individuals' benefit. The second model is similar to the first. It holds that the right to keep and bear arms exists only for individuals actively serving in the militia, and then only pursuant to such regulations as may be prescribed. Under either of the first two models, a private citizen has no right to possess a firearm for personal use…Under this third model, the Second Amendment protects a right of

individuals to own and possess firearms, much as the First Amendment protects a right of individuals to engage in free speech.[14]

The so-called "individual rights" model implies that a law-abiding citizen's right-to-carry a gun must be safeguarded, not just allowed. This model has been codified in two states that allow citizens of proper age to carry weapons without permits: Vermont and Alaska. The individual rights model also gained precedent in a 2001 ruling by the Fifth Circuit Court of Appeals. In *United States v. Emerson*, the court examined the Constitution and the full history of case law and found that the Second Amendment does indeed guarantee individuals the right to keep and bear arms. Building on this ruling, forty-eight states (as of 2007) allowed concealed-carry in some form, with most requiring owners to first obtain licenses. Hence, owning a gun is viewed by most states, and most people in them, as no more of an individual "right" than owning a car or a boat. Knowing that 48 out of 50 states allow citizens to apply for and carry concealed weapons puts LaPierre's constant complaints about the threatened right to carry in a whole new light. While the laws allowing concealed carry have become more and more common, so too have school shootings, a disturbing trend that undercuts LaPierre's claims about violent crime falling with the spread of private gun ownership rights.

Perhaps even more disturbing is that LaPierre has rallied activists to protest that their right to carry is under threat when the right-to-carry has been expanding steadily since the start of the Bush administration. LaPierre has convinced the NRA membership that their right to own guns is under threat, and that they should use their guns as threatening symbols to intimidate political opposition. During the CNN YouTube Democratic Presidential Candidate forum in July 2007, a stone-faced 30-year old named Jered Townsend submitted a video question that had all the markers of LaPierre's argument in *Guns, Freedom, and Terrorism*:

Good evening, America. My name is Jered Townsend from
Clio, Michigan. To all the candidates: tell me your position
on gun control, as myself and other Americans really want
to know if our babies are safe. This is my baby, purchased
under the 1994 gun ban. Please tell me your views. Thank
you.[15]

As Townsend announced in a soft voice, "This is my baby," he held
up a polished, Bushmaster AR15 semiautomatic rifle, then placed it
across his lap, as uncomfortable smiles spread across the candidates'
faces. As a *Detroit Free Press* article would later reveal, Townsend is
the proud owner of "11 to 12" firearms including the Bushmaster
AR15, a weapon manufactured by Colt Firearms and used by the
U.S. military under the name M16.[16] The AR15 is capable of firing
800 .22 rounds per minute, ideal for infantry assault. On the other
hand, when marketed as a sport rifle, the AR15 puts firepower in
the hands of the private citizen that is far beyond appropriate or
necessary levels.

Townsend's YouTube question highlighted a tactic used widely
by the NRA: holding guns during political speech to intimidate and
to cloud the judgment of listeners. The gun, lauded for its value in
protecting the owner from inevitable attack, becomes a symbolic
weapon for protecting the owner from new federal policy. While
Townsend was soft-spoken, and subsequent follow up articles
showed him to be a law-abiding, friendly man, the image that came
across on the screen exuded the threat of violence. In reality, most
citizens do not see assault rifles like the Bushman AR15 as falling
within their Second Amendment rights and, therefore, are in favor
of heavy regulation for limited use in shooting sports, a strategy followed successfully with the passage of an assault weapons ban by the
Clinton administration in 1994, but allowed to lapse by George W.
Bush's Attorney General, John Ashcroft, when it expired in 2004.
The problem the AR15 poses to civic debate is not difficult to see.

A healthy democracy depends on open deliberative conversation between citizens. An American citizen who enters the public square carrying a military assault weapon introduces a troubling and anti-democratic dynamic. The fall of the assault weapons ban and the rise of an era in U.S. history marked by almost universal conceal-carry privileges does more than infuse political debate with the threat and language of violence. It fundamentally alters the model of civics crafted by the founders of the United States that liberated citizens from the command-obedience relationships that defined tyrannical monarchism. Tragically, a tyrannical conception of the individual in American society has reappeared through a string of horrific incidents, such as the mass killings at Columbine High School in 1999 and, more recently, the murders at Virginia Tech in 2007.

Although the killing spree carried out by Seung-Hui Cho in Blacksburg, Virginia had roots in his struggle with mental illness, it also cut a path through the national debate on guns. Taking a pause during his shooting spree, Cho posed for photos of himself brandishing the handguns he used in the massacre, as well as knives and a hammer. As Americans faced the images of a quiet young man posing as a newly emboldened killer holding his weapons, it became clear how Seung-Hui Cho—whether ill or healthy—had turned to guns to give himself a sense of power and dominance over others. The horror that Cho's image evoked was a combination of knowing about the crime he committed, and coming face to face with the individual choice to use gun violence to impose one's will on others.

The scale of the massacre at Virginia Tech was enough to bring LaPierre to the negotiating table with Democrats John Dingell and Carolyn McCarthy to pass a gun bill expanding background checks for new gun buyers. The new law requires states to automate their background check system so that the names of criminals and patients in treatment for mental illness are centralized on a national instant background check system. In response to this legislation, LaPierre said, "We'll work with anyone, if you protect the rights of law-abiding people under the second amendment and you target people that shouldn't have guns."[17] However, LaPierre failed to mention the posting that went up on the NRA website less than twelve hours after the Virginia Tech shootings, calling on the NRA membership to see guns as a form of power in politics, and to stand firm on gun rights even as "the anti-gunners are doing everything they can to chip away at your rights."[18]

3. DEATH BY IMMIGRATION

On August 25, 2006, Pat Buchanan appeared on FOX News' *Your World with Neil Cavuto* to discuss the invasion of "saboteurs" that threatened to destroy America. The occasion of the interview was the publication of Buchanan's latest book, *State of Emergency: The Third World Invasion and Conquest of America.* The subject discussed was immigration:

> I think it is the most important domestic issue in the country. It almost equals Iraq in the minds of the American people. Neil, I think it is going to be an issue in 2006, in 2008, and for the rest of our lifetimes, because Tom Tancredo is exactly right. America is in an existential crisis. I mean, the president himself admits, 6 million tried to break in across the border on his watch. By my count, 500,000 make it every year, which means 2.5 million have invaded. There are spies in there, undoubtedly saboteurs in there, probably al Qaeda, probably Hezbollah. And, if the president does not build that security fence on the border, and he grants amnesty, the whole world is coming, and this is going to be the end of the United States as people

of my generation who grew up in another country knew it.[1]

Immigration, claimed Buchanan, is an issue that "almost equals Iraq," suggesting that the illegal movement of Latinos into the United States is a danger on par with the violent overthrow of the Middle East by radical groups luring children to strap bombs to their chests and then detonate them in crowds. In fact, compared to terrorism, Buchanan suggested that immigration was a far greater threat to the survival of America, and certainly one that had a longer history and more steady, destructive impact. The issue was not simply infiltration of immigrant communities by al Qaeda, although Buchanan made sure to float that fear as well. The problem is that immigration across America's southern border threatens the survival of the racial balance between a white majority and African-American minority that Buchanan claimed has defined the United States since its beginnings. The immigration crisis, as Buchanan espouses it, is a rerun of the great barbarian conquest that destroyed Rome and threatened China. According to his violent imagination, immigration will eradicate America if government does not muster enough political will to build the Great Wall—or rather, the Great Fence—spanning the entire length of the southern border.

Many Americans believe Pat Buchanan is little more than a museum piece among contemporary right-wing pundits, but he is one of the most influential sources of violent rhetoric in the media today. Even though it has become de rigueur of late to credit Lou Dobbs with the dubious distinction of moving the immigration debate to hostile, nationalist ground, the most disruptive and persistent voice on the issue has been, and continues to be, Buchanan. Despite not having his own show on TV or radio, Buchanan has become a fixture on MSNBC and elsewhere, often appearing on two or three different shows during the same day to hawk his arguments about the immigrant invasion and the impending destruction of American civilization. Moreover, his broadcast media presence is not limited in any way to shows that are identifiably right-wing, as Buchanan is a regular on *The McLaughlin Report* and *Hardball With Chris Matthews*, in addition to his appearances on Tucker Carlson's show.

Although a presence in the right-wing ideological movement since the Nixon era, Buchanan burst onto the national scene in the early 1990s with a presidential campaign that combined explicit talk of racial separation, economic protectionism and anti-immigration policy. A clever political tactician and a powerful speechwriter, Buchanan was twice able to turn the New Hampshire Republican presidential primary into a vehicle for promoting his retro racial populism. Running against George H. W. Bush in 1992, Buchanan turned a few short weeks of dazzling speeches into 38 percent of the primary vote, placing him a close second. The New Hampshire results and his persistent campaigning landed him a coveted spot as a keynote speaker at the 1992 Republican National Convention, where he delivered the lines that would subsequently define his entire career:

> My friends, this election is about much more than who gets what. It is about what we believe. It is about what we stand for as Americans. There is a religious war going on in our country for the soul of America. It is a cultural war, as critical to the kind of nation we will one day be as the Cold War itself. And in that struggle for the soul of America, Clinton & Clinton are on the other side, and George Bush is on our side.[2]

Curiously, the Pat Buchanan of 1992 had not yet applied his violent rhetoric to the topic of immigration. In the first campaign against Bush, the focus of Buchanan's economic populism was a perfect storm of liberal evils that threatened the well-being of what he claimed as traditional America: abortion, environmentalism, and the gay rights movement. By listing these issues as battles in a "war," Buchanan reframed political debate as a violent clash between liberal and conservative armies. In fact, Buchanan's metaphorical concept of "politics [as] war" was a clever inversion of a famous observation by eighteenth century German military historian Carl von Clausewitz: "War is politics pursued by other means."[3] By writing about "war" in terms of "politics," Clausewitz made the violent actions of war seem intellectual and controllable.[4] By presenting "politics" in terms of cultural "war," Buchanan achieved the opposite effect, making the discursive process of democracy seem life threatening and dangerous. To rally the Republican Party to this idea of a religious and cultural war, Buchanan did not look to immigration, but to Nixon's old canard of law and order in a time of racial tension. He invoked the image of racial violence during the Los Angeles riots to remind Republicans that abortion, environmentalism, and gay rights were the newest fronts in a "war" that could only be won through street-level military battles. He closed his speech with a description of soldiers who fought to save Los Angeles from "the mob." Buchanan assured his audience that only one thing could guarantee the future of America: "Force, rooted in justice, backed by courage."

Buchanan's nationalist rhetoric was steeped initially in a relatively straightforward economic populism. The doom he prophesized in 1992 was working Americans' unemployment due to the war waged by liberal extremists who cared more about "insects, rats and birds," than families. When he ran for president again four years later, he revised his idea of the culture war to focus on a new battle and a new enemy. Instead of environmentalists, Buchanan warned that the threat against American working families was immigrants, and that the new battle was not just for jobs, but for racial survival against our enemies at the southern border:

> Three months ago I talked…to a young border Patrol agent. He had been decorated as a hero. He showed me the back of his head. There was a scar all over it. Illegal aliens had crossed the border, he went to apprehend them, and they waited to trap him. When he walked into their trap, they

smashed his head with a rock and came to kill him. Only when he took out his gun and fired in self-defense did his friends come and save his life. Yet our leaders, timid and fearful of being called names, do nothing. Well, they have not invented the name I have not been called. So, the Custodians of Political Correctness do not frighten me. And I will do what is necessary to defend the borders of my country even it means putting the National Guard all along our southern frontier.[5]

Buchanan was telling his followers that they needed to guard America from two dangerous forces: the undocumented aliens sneaking across the border with the intent of smashing people to death with rocks, and—just as bad—the "Custodians of Political Correctness" (a.k.a., liberals) who had, somehow, paralyzed the entire U.S. government with such fear that it refused to stop said rock brandishing killers from storming across the Rio Grande. A vote for Buchanan was thus a vote to call in the cavalry—a vote not only for protectionist, economic populism, but for armed confrontation as the only viable path to American survival.

After his third unsuccessful bid for the presidency in 2000, Buchanan turned from giving speeches laced with racial nationalism to writing books that elaborated racial nationalist theories of civilization. His initial attempt to transform the violent, anti-immigration rhetoric of his 1996 and 2000 presidential bids into an ideological anchor for a new conservative revolution was his 2002 book *Death of the West: How Dying Populations And Immigrant Invasions Imperil Our Country and Civilization*. The title *Death of the West* sums up most of what the book contains: namely, a nationalist call to arms—both ideological arms and literal arms—rooted in the pseudo-scientific conclusion that current immigration from Latin American to the United States, and from North Africa to Europe, are invasions by inferior races bent on the destruction of European and American civilization. While Buchanan describes Spanish and Arabic speaking immigrants as if they are barbarian hordes screaming across the border, he blames the situation on liberal multiculturalism, belief in equality, abortion rights and environmentalism.

The fate America and Europe face, however, is worse than merely political minority status. According to Buchanan, immigrants who have more children than their host-country counterparts threaten to bring about the slow "genocide" and cultural extermination of European and American civilization. "This is not a matter of prophecy," Buchanan writes in *Death of the West*. It is a question "of mathematics."[6] Buchanan presents immigration through the most violent scenario imaginable: genocide argued as if it were a scientific certainty. The violent framing of immigration as a force threatening to literally kill America's and Europe's future is the smokescreen that hides Buchanan's main thesis in *Death of the West*, which is that the Unites States is not a country founded on the principle of equality, but on the idea that the majority will, and should, be subservient to a "natural aristocracy:"

> What America is about is not equality of condition or equality of result, but freedom, so a "natural aristocracy" of ability, achievement, virtue and excellence—from athletics to the arts to the academy—can rise to lead, inspire, and set an example for us all to follow and a mark for us all to aim at.[7]

Nobody should be lulled into believing that Buchanan's economic populism even vaguely resembles a call for economic equality. While his reference to the idea of a "natural aristocracy" draws on a vague concept that Thomas Jefferson toyed with in a series of letters he wrote to John Adams, it is a red-herring in Buchanan's book. Jefferson only used the idea to distinguish between an aristocracy found on birth and wealth (e.g., "artificial") and one supposedly rooted in talent (e.g., "natural"). Indeed, Jefferson's contribution to American history was to build a Constitution that guarded against the rise of aristocracies and sought a balance between participatory egalitarianism at the local level, and deliberative representation in government. Buchanan distorts Jefferson's words into a credo against immigration and multiculturalism. The sleight of hand in Buchanan's anti-immigration rhetoric is his deft use of violent rhetoric and patriotic references to the founding fathers to lull his reader into thinking that he supports egalitarian workers rights. A closer look at what Buchanan actually says, however, reveals the disturbing logic beneath the rhetoric—a logic that brands egalitarianism as the ideological force causing the violent overthrow of American culture and society.

While ostensibly about immigration, *The Death of the West* was really Buchanan's idiosyncratic attempt to re-orient American politics to a long-since defunct superstition called "degeneration," which was one of the many pseudo-intellectual neuroses that drove nineteenth century European nationalists to conclude that their countries were in the late stages of cultural death. They were not, of course, but such paranoid fear fueled the rise of some of the most horrific nationalist projects in history. In *The Death of the West*, Buchanan embraces "degeneration" as a shorthand explanation for his much more long-winded idea that liberal approaches to education, health, law, government and business have been steadily destroying America since the start of the twentieth century:

> The era of sex, booze, and jazz led naturally to the era of sex, drugs, and rock and roll. Only the degeneration was briefly interrupted by the intrusive reality of Depression, World War, and Cold War.[8]

By describing American liberalism as a social bacchanalia of jazz and gin, Buchanan sets up his broader argument that Americans have become too drunk, sexed, and distracted to notice the barbarian hordes rushing across the southern border with packs on their backs and "La Reconquista" on their minds. Because liberals have waged a "war against the past" that has destroyed America's national memory, nobody truly understands the force driving waves of Latino immigrants across the border.[9] What motivates them, according to Buchanan, is not jobs, education, healthcare, or general security for their families, but a desire for revenge. For nearly two centuries, writes Buchanan, the citizens of Latin America in general, and Mexico in particular, have been looking north with an eye towards avenging the defeat of General Santa Anna, which led to the independence of Texas.

Framing Mexican immigration as revenge for a 160-year old military defeat, however, is only one part of Buchanan's violent rhetoric. The next part comes in his 2006 book, *State of Emergency*, where he brings Samuel Huntington's "The Clash of Civilizations?" into his argument about La Reconquista.[10] The Ur text of pundits seeking to recast cultural diversity as violent confrontation between cultures, Huntington argued provocatively that the great source of conflict in the twenty first century would not be economic or ideological, but cultural. With its overt use of a war metaphor, Huntington's essay pushed conservative intellectuals to frame their ideas about new global tensions as a "battle" between "civilizations" vying for survival:

> It is my hypothesis that the fundamental source of conflict in this new world will not be primarily ideological or primarily economic. The great divisions among humankind and the dominating source of conflict will be cultural. Nation states will remain the most powerful actors in world affairs, but the principal conflicts of global politics will occur between nations and groups of different civilizations. The clash of civilizations will dominate global politics. The fault lines between civilizations will be the battle lines of the future.[11]

Buchanan not only uses Huntington's hypothesis in both of his books on immigration, but he uses his words, too. "Civilization" is in the subtitle of *The Death of the West*. In *State of Emergency*, civilization is not only in the first chapter title ("How Civilizations Perish"), but also the first word of the text. Beyond "The Clash of Civilizations?" Buchanan also draws from Huntington's November 2000 essay about Mexico, quoting the piece in both *The Death of the West* and *State of Emergency*:

> If over one million Mexican soldiers crossed the border Americans would treat it as a major threat to their national security and react accordingly. The invasion of over one million Mexican civilians, as [President] Fox seems to recommend, would be a comparable threat to American societal security, and Americans should react against it with vigor.[12]

The subtle change between *Death of the West* and *State of Emergency* speaks to Buchanan's rhetorical agenda with regard to immigration. In *The Death Of The West*, Buchanan describes Mexican immigrants as haunted by the national memory of defeat in nineteenth century Texas. This memory, Buchanan would have us believe, drives them across the border to conquer American jobs. In *State of Emergency*, Buchanan kicks up the "conquest" concept a few notches, reworking it into the more menacing idea of a Mexican militaristic movement driven by a quest to retake "Aztlán"—a mythical name 1970s Chicano activists gave to the land that Mexico ceded to the United States in the Mexican-American War. Huntington's rhetoric about the "invasion" of Mexican immigrants provides Buchanan a violent image for distinguishing between all prior immigrant groups who have come to America with an eye towards assimilation, and those who come here to conquer.

Critics often point to Buchanan's ambiguous views about race and Adolf Hitler to critique his rhetoric, although that critique draws attention away from Buchanan's use of violent language.[13] While Buchanan's arguments about immigration, for example, do reference race, the key focus in his rhetoric is a narrative of violent struggle between Latino and American civilizations. As such, Buchanan may be racist, but in the sense of Victorian manifest destiny theories, not in the sense of World War II era fascist dictators. Buchanan is not concerned with separating races within American society, nor does he blame social ills on the biological mixing of races through marriage and reproduction, which was the hallmark belief of the various, racist fascisms that bloomed in the early twentieth century and which led to such moral aberrations as the Nazi extermination camps. Instead, Buchanan turns the late twentieth century critique of racism on its head, arguing that western guilt over "Hitler's crimes" have lulled America and Europe into letting their guard down.[14] Buchanan would have us believe that seeing the world in terms of distinct, hierarchical races with white Europeans at the top is not a problem, unless one commits crimes based on that belief. Those who critique racism are misguided in Buchanan's eyes because their concern gets in the way of racial common sense. By contrast, Buchanan admires those post-World War II politicians and intellectuals who have been willing to return to the concept of race without fear of being branded atavistic by liberals. In a recent installment of his syndicated column, for example, Buchanan expressed admiration for Nobel Prize winning geneticist and discoverer of the double helix James Watson for precisely this reason. As he wondered aloud as to why a planned lecture by Watson had been cancelled, Buchanan cast a bright light on his own view of race and racism:

> Did he defend the chattel slavery in which five of our first seven presidents engaged? No. Did he agree with Abraham Lincoln that blacks did not deserve equal social and political rights and should be sent back to the continent whence their ancestors came? No. Did he argue for the segregation that was the law in the nation's capital in which this writer

grew up? No. Did he utter the "N-word" used by Harry Truman, who integrated the armed forces, and Lyndon Johnson, who enacted the Civil Rights Act of 1964 and Voting Rights Act of 1965? No...He had simply told the *Sunday Times* he was "inherently gloomy about the prospects of Africa" because "all our social policies are based on the fact that their intelligence is the same as ours—whereas all the testing says not really."[15]

Even though Watson himself apologized for his misguided remark, Buchanan still embraced it. Liberal fear of racism is contributing to the death of Western civilization, Buchanan surmised, not a few observations about race made by a scientist. Watson's critics should have apologized, according to Buchanan, not Watson.

And yet, racism does not seem to be the driving force behind Buchanan's ideas so much as his violent conception of immigration and its consequences. Accordingly, one of Buchanan's heroes, about whom he writes in glowing terms in *State of Emergency*, is Enoch Powell , a once prominent member of the British Conservative Party who fell from grace after delivering a 1968 speech forewarning that apocalyptic consequences would result from too much immigration from the Commonwealth countries into Great Britain. Often dubbed the "Rivers of Blood" speech for its vivid reference to a metaphor of war used in Virgil's *Aeneid*, Powell sounded the alarm that England was in the process of being overrun by black immigrants who were not only incapable of integration into British society, but also battered the elderly. Powell concluded with a prophesy of Britain's violent demise as a result of too much concern for fighting racism:

> For these dangerous and divisive elements the legislation proposed in the Race Relations Bill is the very pabulum they need to flourish. Here is the means of showing that the immigrator [sic] communities can organize to consolidate

their members, to agitate and campaign against their fellow citizens, and to overawe and dominate the rest with the legal weapons which the ignorant and the ill-informed have provided. As I look ahead, I am filled with foreboding; like the Roman, I seem to see "the River Tiber foaming with much blood." That tragic and intractable phenomenon which we watch with horror on the other side of the Atlantic but which there is interwoven with the history and existence of the States itself, is coming upon us here by our own volition and our own neglect. Indeed, it has all but come.[16]

Buchanan quotes Powell's "Rivers of Blood" speech at the start of a chapter titled "Eurasia," in which he describes how Arabic-speaking North African immigrants are, supposedly, re-conquering Europe. For Buchanan, Powell's great accomplishment was his willingness to define immigration in racial terms and then link it to the impending death of British society. The problem with Buchanan's admiration is that nearly a half-century after Powell predicted Britain's demise, that downfall has not come. Buchanan overlooks the fact that time has proved Powell's prophecy false.

Despite the logical flaws in Buchanan's racial nationalism, his rhetoric about immigration continues to flow directly into mainstream political debate through an endless series of television appearances. Turn on your television at just about any time of the day, any day of the week, and Pat Buchanan is there, and has been there for nearly a quarter century.

The issue shouted down by the violent language in Buchanan's immigration rhetoric is "trade." The debate is about moral trade strategies versus a U.S. policy that harms the lives of workers and damages the environment.

Buchanan's violent vision of a two-fronted war against Western civilization is more than just a throwback to past theories of white racial supremacy. His vision acts as a poison pill to one of the most important debates of our day, the discussion about the the North American Free Trade Agreement (NAFTA). Proponents of NAFTA hold it up as the triumphant accomplishment of "free trade," which is an economically and morally ambiguous concept. In theory, if there are no barriers to commerce and trade in North America, poverty will diminish, joblessness will end, and violent crime will decrease. NAFTA has not only failed to live up to these promises, but has contributed to two key changes that have been detrimental to living standards for millions of people: the bankrupting of family farming in Latin America, and the elimination of vast segments of the manufacturing sector in the United States. Immigration from Latin America, and frustration in the United States in reaction to it, has nothing to do with "conquest," as Buchanan believed, but by the increasing need of rural Mexican farm workers to find work, and the pressure in American communities to maintain a standard of living once held in place by manufacturing jobs. These two key changes together form one of the most important political stories of our time, but that story is barely audible above Buchanan's constant narrative on the death of American civilization at the hands of an immigrant invasion.

At its most primary, political level, America's immigration problem is a product of what David Sirota has aptly named the "hostile takeover" of key economic policies in our government by vast corporations in control of unimaginable wealth.[17] The takeover process has slowly undone the kind of government that America enjoyed from roughly the time of Theodore Roosevelt through the presidency of Jimmy Carter. During this period, the government maintained the upper hand against private power by leveraging the collective resources of the country towards economic policies that were beneficial—in the short and long term—to a majority of Americans. The slow unraveling of regulations on powerful private interests began in earnest in the 1980s, with Ronald Reagan's idea that lowering taxes would increase the general welfare of the nation. Reagan followed this misdirected notion with vast deregulation of the system of banking oversights and checks that had helped to protect people's savings since the market crash of the late 1920s. Accordingly, private interests began to grow increasingly powerful again and, ultimately, led to the collapse of the savings and loan industry during the presidency of George H. W. Bush. Unlike previous periods of history where Democratic presidents had curtailed the rise of powerful private interests, Bill Clinton's administration did not push back in any significant way.

Reagan's gutting of the federal regulations that protected American savings was based on the purely theoretical, partisan idea that government was bad because it hindered "free markets." The theory that economic markets can exist without any rules, however, does not make logical sense. If rules are not set in advance, then the strongest player sets them by default. Rules define how any game should unfold and the same is true for economics. Rather than an economic system in the best interest of all citizens, talk of "free markets" is Republican framing that advances an eighteenth century idea that government should be an instrument controlled by the wealthiest segment of society, who then rule over the rest of the population. Seeking to advance this ideological economics in the midst of a global recession, President George H. W. Bush, along with Canadian Prime Minister Brian Mulroney and Mexican President Carlos Salinas de Gortari, signed NAFTA in 1992. The new treaty promised to turn the entire continent into one free market of unregulated economic success. The agreement was the logical evolution of Reagan's national "free market" frame into a new global "free trade" frame. Whereas "free market" reforms were based on the elimination of banking regulations and taxes, "free trade" was based on the relaxation of labor laws, tariffs, and environmental standards. Just as Reagan's deregulations had ushered in a new ease with which U.S. government officials could be wined and dined by corporate lobbyists, NAFTA brought about a new system of backroom negotiations between captains of industry and heads of state.

The end of this story is not hard to figure out. NAFTA did not fulfill what its proponents promised. The middle class did not expand significantly in Latin American countries. Wealth did not trickle down to working class communities in the United States. Poverty was not alleviated on a vast scale. Crime did not end. For the economy, "free trade" resulted in an increased consolidation of wealth. In government, "free trade" gave rise to a new political argument that elected officials who opposed "free trade" were endangering freedom itself. As a result of NAFTA, U.S. manufacturing relocated to Mexico in search of cheap labor. A less well-known result is the story of what happened to the Mexican corn industry. In her essay "Migration and Corn," Sally Kohn describes how NAFTA ripped through the small-hold Mexican corn industry, turning millions of small-farm workers into out-of-work people:

> In all, 18 million Mexicans, including farmers and their families, rely on corn for their livelihood. Enter NAFTA in 1994, which opened the U.S.-Mexico border to trade. It's worth noting that before the wealthy nations in the European Union like France and Germany expanded trade with poorer nations like Portugal and Greece, the wealthier countries first transferred huge sums of money to the poorer nations, to build their infrastructure and help get them to the equal footing necessary for trade to work. Not so with Mexico. The United States (1990 GDP: $23,130 –a.k.a. Goliath) became "equal trading partners" with Mexico (1990 GDP: $6,090 –a.k.a. David)…An estimated two million family farmers who can't compete with subsidized U.S. corn have been driven from their land. They now have to buy imported corn to feed their families but don't have the income to afford it.[18]

The idea that Mexican immigrants cross the border as part of a broad-scale scheme of conquest and revenge seems ludicrous in the face of Kohn's chilling description of how NAFTA wrecked the lives of millions of corn farmers. To truly understand why so many rural Mexicans migrate to the United States in search of work to feed their families, the key is corn. La Reconquista? Not even close. Kohn's discussion of Mexican corn workers dispossessed of their livelihood by large, U.S. agra-business reads like the old time tales of downtrodden workers in company towns, where mass inequalities between business owners and labor gave rise to the union movement and the progressive era of worker protections. At the beginning of the twentieth century, Teddy Roosevelt broke the iron grip that industrial barons held over the rest of America; a few decades later, Franklin Roosevelt broke the grip of banking barons. In those waves of progressive reforms, a new era was ushered in whereby government stood between citizens and the private interests that sought to exploit. At the beginning of the twenty-first century, by contrast, private interests once again have citizens to exploit—this time in Mexico—and the U.S. government is no longer preventing this exploitation. It is in fact the catalyst setting it in motion. We are back where we started over 100 years ago.

How government became an agent of private interests to the detriment of corn farmers in Mexico is not a mystery. Private companies hired lobbyists to press for their interests so that those companies could to profit from government. As Sherrod Brown describes in *Myths of Free Trade*:

> From 1979 to 1994, registered foreign agents—American citizens representing foreign concerns and lobbying the U.S. Congress or executive branch—increased eightfold! Since then the numbers have continued to grow, and it is not only foreign countries these lobbyists represent. Literally thousands of American attorneys, former government officials, former congressmen and senators, and others represent American corporations that are doing business

abroad and foreign companies doing business in the United States and looking for special treatment from Congress. In this supercharged world of foreign-bought and corporate-owned influence, ordinary Americans don't get much of a hearing.[19]

These "foreign agents" were lobbyists hired by foreign companies to make sure "free trade" benefited their employers. According to Brown, Reagan's presidency witnessed the rise of government as a revolving door to big business. In this time period, the people in charge of agencies created to protect American citizens began accepting jobs from businesses seeking to use their knowledge and expertise to subvert the very agencies they were once charged with managing. It is surprising, given all the media coverage of "illegal aliens," that one never hears the phrase "foreign agents" used on TV to describe the global economic crisis and its direct impact on Americans. That is because the immigrant conquest theories of pundits like Pat Buchanan drown out any discussion of private interests both at home and abroad that use cash to buy favors from the U.S. government. Just as American agricultural big business employed lobbyists to drive the Mexican corn farmer into poverty, a string of foreign governments have hired foreign agents since the 1980s. As economist Pat Choate once observed, the problem is not just that former U.S. government employees are hired by foreign governments to do a job, but that these foreign agents "proceed as if they had a fiduciary and ethical responsibility to help their client win at all costs, even when winning for a foreign company or government runs counter to the interests of the nation."[20]

Foreign nations should not be banned from conducting business in the United States any more than U.S. companies should be barred from pursuing business interests abroad. And yet, the propagandistic notion of "free trade" has given rise to a system of influence peddling and trade agreements that have tipped the American economy into a crisis. Instead of advancing ethical business practices abroad, structures like NAFTA send American companies chasing down unethical business conditions in foreign countries. As a result, American businesses, by and large, do not seek to build sustainable business models based on sound labor and environmental practices, but instead bank their profit margins on being able to intimidate foreign governments into relaxing labor or environmental laws that might add to manufacturing costs.

To swing the civic debate back towards pragmatic solutions to the problems created by free market economics and free trade treaties, the public discussion must shift away from fears of cultural destruction to the economics that effect our everyday lives. Economist and *New York Times* editorialist Paul Krugman wrote recently, for example, that the solution to the problem of low wages and environmental damage caused by free trade agreements from the 1990s is not to end trade altogether, but to strengthen the "social safety net."[21] Krugman's belief is that increased trade can benefit society only when citizens of all nations are guaranteed the basic necessities that guarantee their longevity, quality of life, and piece of mind, such as education, healthcare, wage standards, job safety and pensions. Economic experts—and pundits—initiating a conversation about "social safety" is both welcome and familiar, as it was the basic progressive conversation that marked the beginning of the twentieth century.

4. LOTS OF 9/11'S

On October 13, 2003, Ann Coulter appeared on *Hannity & Colmes* together with John MacArthur, the publisher of *Harper's* magazine. The topic of discussion was MacArthur's article, "Impeach Bush Now," in which he argued that a wide range of events surrounding the President—including lying to Congress and outing a covert CIA agent—had made the case for issuing articles of impeachment much stronger. The conversation began, as they typically do on *Hannity & Colmes*, with Sean Hannity insulting the liberal guest, after which he brought Coulter into the mix:

> COULTER: You don't impeach for disagreements over policy. It is for misbehavior; that is what misdemeanor means. It's for bad decorum.
> COLMES: Ann, we didn't let Rick make a speech. You can't make a speech, either.
> COULTER: Well, actually, you did.
> COLMES: I know it's hard, but if you look to your left, I know that's difficult. Look, I don't think he should be impeached. I disagree with Rick about that.
> COULTER: That's very big of you.

COLMES: Thank you. I think I'd rather put our time and effort toward 2004, and just like I don't think Bill Clinton should have been impeached, I don't. But I understand Rick's point. There are many Americans who increasingly seem to feel that we were not leveled with, for whatever reason, whether it was Bush who did it or people in his administration who gave him false information. He did say the IAEA reported that Iraq was six months away from a nuclear capability, which turned out not to be true.[1] It's a scare tactic.

COULTER: He got the name of the institute wrong.

COLMES: Saying "I misspoke," and they said they misspoke about a number of things. Misspoke about uranium. They misspoke about tubes, misspoke about how many things.

MACARTHUR: Right.

COLMES: Misspoke lets him off the hook?

COULTER: No. Liberals don't want to fight terrorism. You want there to be lots of 9/11's.[2]

Although it may not seem clear at first glance, this exchange has more in common with the games between the Harlem Globetrotters and the Washington Generals than with an actual political debate. *Hannity & Colmes* is television entertainment dressed up as political debate, but unlike the Globetrotters, the show is not funny and always comes back to the same theme: that liberals betray America. In this vaudeville of violent rhetoric, Hannity plays the role of the loud conservative, while Colmes plays the meek liberal. Needless to say, the loud one always wins. The guests change, the topics shift, but the game is always rigged, and Coulter always performs well for the lights. In the exchange with MacArthur, Coulter wielded what became her signature move in the run-up to the re-election of George W. Bush—the rhetorical equivalent of a hook shot from mid-court. Cornered by Colmes and MacArthur on the question of Bush's lies, Coulter threw a quick head fake with the idea that Bush merely "misspoke," then suddenly tossed up the accusation that liberals want more mass murder—"lots of 9/11's." Despite being the cheapest of cheap shots, it still scored. And like every great performer, Coulter made it look effortless.

Live television happens too fast for most of us to analyze the kind of whiplash rhetorical move that Coulter executed in this exchange, but the transcript gives the freeze frame we need to understand it. Colmes asks Coulter, "Misspoke lets him off the hook?" Coulter replies, "No. Liberals don't want to fight terrorism. You want there to be lots of 9/11's." Despite the fact that it bears no relation to any reality, Coulter's line is a slam dunk on shock value alone. Treason trumps perjury.

In October 2003, American nerves were still raw from the deaths at the Pentagon and the World Trade Center. Ground Zero was still an infected wound a few miles from the FOX News studios. It would take three more years before Coulter would feel bold enough to accuse widows of the men who died in the attacks of "enjoying their husbands' deaths." But that night on *Hannity and Colmes*, she was using a technique she had been practicing for some time.

As a political correspondent for the conservative weekly *Human Events*, Coulter had started making occasional appearances on CNBC's show *Equal Time* in mid-1997. It was her role as one of several right-wing attorneys secretly advising Paula Jones, however, that rocketed her to pundit fame.[3] Discussing the Clinton scandal with *Newsweek* reporter Michael Isikoff, Coulter revealed that she had spread a false rumor to the media that President Clinton suffered from Peyronie's disease, an obscure syndrome leading to the disfigurement of the penis. According to Isikoff, Coulter leaked the story to the *New York Post* in September of 1997 with the claim that Clinton's Peyronie's disease was in fact the "distinguishing characteristic" of the "presidential penis" that Paula Jones was supposedly able to identify to prove that Clinton had exposed himself to her.[4] While rumor of the "distinguishing characteristic" had been circulating in the press since 1994, Coulter leaked the false Peyronie's disease claim in 1997 as part of a strategy to prevent Clinton from settling with Jones.[5] With Coulter's persistence, the story eventually aired on the *Don Imus Show* and in the *Washington Times*.[6] More importantly, it put Coulter on TV, where she played the peculiar role of a legal expert who discussed the details of the president's supposed genital disfigurement.

For Coulter, Clinton's troubles showcased her willingness to blurt out sexually shocking lines with the flare of a sarcastic teenager mouthing off to a teacher. Her first breakthrough moment was a TV appearance on CNBC's *Rivera Live* on October 15, 1997, the same day she leaked the Peyronie's story to the press. During the exchange about the Paula Jones case with Geraldo Rivera and a Democratic Party activist, Stanton Gildenhorn, Coulter introduced the topic of Peyronie's disease:

> COULTER: Peyronie's disease, and it's only apparent when in a state of arousal. A urologist would not have seen that unless there's something wrong.
> RIVERA: What is that disease again? It sounded something dental. What was that? Per...
> COULTER: Unless—well, I'm not really sure how much I can say on TV.
> RIVERA: Well, what's the name of it?
> COULTER: Peyronie's disease.
> RIVERA: Peyronie's disease.
> GILDENHORN: Now this was all reported...
> COULTER: It means it's bent when erect.[7]

Rivera ended the exchange by gleefully proclaiming that Coulter's comments had turned his show into "*Penthouse* forum." As Coulter divulged to Isikoff years later, none of the Peyronie's disease exchange was spontaneous. Beyond the smears of Clinton, Coulter used the Rivera broadcasts as a platform for selling her subsequent book on Clinton, *High Crimes and Misdemeanors: The Case Against Bill Clinton*. The key to Coulter's success during her *Rivera Live* appearances, which continued for several months, was her ability to mix legalistic political diatribe against liberals with sexual detail about Clinton's body, a combination that put her on the short list of top conservative pundits. But even as Coulter mixed constitutional jargon with references to male genitalia, she was testing new rhetoric that veered away from sex to accuse liberals of murder. In the book on Clinton, for example, Coulter devoted an entire chapter to her "Fostergate" conspiracy theory, through which she speculated that long time friend and close associate of the Clintons, Vince Foster, had been murdered in the woods on the orders of the sitting President.

As the Clinton impeachment hysteria and sales of her book died down, Coulter's rhetoric settled squarely on violence. Her new style of sadistic humor continued to drive readership to her columns and viewers to her TV appearances. Similar to the way she seized on the Clinton scandal to carve out her niche on broadcast political talk shows, Coulter used the story of the terrorist attacks in 2001 to maintain her position at the top of the pundit charts. In her September 12, 2001 column "This is War," which she penned hours after the planes struck, Coulter stepped fully into the violent rhetoric that would define her for the duration of the Bush-Cheney years. The column is still powerful to read, and not simply for its shock value. Critics of Coulter often make the mistake of saying that she is not a good writer, but they are wrong. Like so many pundits, her strength as a writer lies in her ability to turn a sharp phrase. "This is War" starts out with a heart-felt celebration of Coulter's friend and conservative colleague Barbara Olson, who was killed on the plane that hit the Pentagon. The writing showcased Coulter's gift for using unfiltered boldness:

Barbara Olsen kept her cool. In the hysteria and terror of

hijackers herding passengers to the rear of the plane, she retrieved her cell phone and called her husband, Ted, the Solicitor General of the United States. Barbara was still on the phone with Ted when her plane plunged in a fiery explosion directly into the Pentagon. Barbara risked having her neck slit to warn the country of a terrorist attack. She was a patriot to the very end.[8]

Despite this eloquent opening, the column quickly turns ugly. Having started with a gutsy tribute to a friend, Coulter closed with a call for war that mimicked the violent rhetoric of medieval crusaders:

We should invade their countries, kill their leaders and convert them to Christianity. We weren't punctilious about locating and punishing only Hitler and his top officers. We carpet-bombed German cities; we killed civilians. That's war. And this is war.[9]

The impact of her column's conclusion was overwhelming. Coulter's call for the assassination of heads of state turned a tribute to her lost friend into a media firestorm about herself. Nobody sounded the alarm louder than her own publishers. After reading the piece, readers of the *National Review Online* (NRO) the most prominent conservative journal that carried Coulter's column, responded with strong criticism of her calls to "invade...kill...and convert" Muslim countries. Coulter reacted in kind. According to Jonah Goldberg, then NRO editor at large, Coulter's response to her critics set in motion a series of events that led to her leaving the magazine:

In the wake of her invade-and-Christianize-them column, Coulter wrote a long, rambling rant of a response to her critics that was barely coherent...Running this "piece" would have been an embarrassment to Ann, and to NRO. Rich Lowry pointed this out to her in an e-mail (I was returning from my honeymoon). She wrote back an angry response, defending herself from the charge that she hates Muslims and wants to convert them at gunpoint. But this was not the point. It was NEVER the point. The problem with Ann's first column was its sloppiness of expression and thought. Ann didn't fail as a person—as all her critics on the Left say—she failed as WRITER, which for us is almost as bad...What's Ann's take on all this? Well, she told the *Washington Post* yesterday that she loves it, because she's gotten lots of great publicity. That pretty much sums Ann up.[10]

"L'Affair Coulter," as Goldberg dubbed it ironically, was more than a soap opera between the NRO and Coulter. It delineated a new boundary between Coulter and conservative establishment writers—a boundary that she would continue to exploit.

The episode with the NRO shows, among other things, that after Coulter was hired as a brash lawyer willing to discuss false details of Clinton's sexuality on live television, the conservative media circuit expected her to continue playing that role for a while. Instead, Coulter treated the prestige of the NRO and the nation's emotional wounds after 9/11 as fair game to catapult herself into the role of America's most vulgar pundit. And she made lots and lots of money as a result. Perhaps the biggest cash cow to come out of her rise to the top was her 2003 book *Treason: Liberal Treachery From the Cold War To The War on Terrorism*, in which she argued that the American left had been fighting and concealing its designs to destroy America for over half a century.

Formidable and unnerving in live interviews, Coulter is much more mechanistic and predictable in print, to the point of repetition. Nonetheless, what gives her the confidence to argue on TV comes from the rhetorical moves she rehearses in her books. She used *High Crimes* to claim that the basis for impeachment was the vague and politically malleable concept of "misbehavior." Coulter then went on to use the "misbehavior" argument in her book to claim that the lascivious one-liners she threw out about Clinton were actual evidence for constitutional action. The difficulty in arguing with Coulter, in other words, runs much deeper than just her unflappable spoiledteenager sneers or her willingness to swamp any policy debate with accusations that liberals long for the mass murder of Americans. Everything that Coulter says about liberals wanting terrorists to win the war on terror and liberals hating America, for example, is based on an idea laid out clearly in *Treason*, but it is not an idea about terrorists or Islam. The broad frame for all her arguments about liberals and terrorism is her theory that Franklin Roosevelt's administration supported murderous foreign regimes and gave control of the U.S. government to communist spies. This is the key to everything she says about terrorism, because Coulter is not just arguing that liberals oppose Bush's policies; she is arguing that liberals are pathologically opposed to America, and have been so since at least the first half of the twentieth century:

> Liberals have a preternatural gift for striking a position on the side of treason. You could be talking about Scrabble and they would instantly leap to the anti-American position. Everyone says liberals love America, too. No they don't. Whenever the nation is under attack, from within or without, liberals side with the enemy. This is their essence. The left's obsession with the crimes of the West and their Rousseauian respect for Third World savages all flow from this subversive goal. If anyone has the gaucherie to point out the left's nearly unblemished record of rooting against America, liberals turn around and scream "McCarthyism!"[11]

Coulter grounds her arguments about liberals and terrorism, in other words, in the idea that liberals always have (1) sought the defeat of America, (2) helped aid the victory of America's enemies, and (3) been particularly supportive of those enemies with a record of mass murder. Like all exaggerated and false claims advanced for shock value, this one is easy to debunk. But the key is realizing that these are not just through away one-liners, but strategic statements that establish broad logical frames. Thus, while Coulter's antics infuriate her critics, they create rhetorical openings for her to make further outlandish claims.

According to Coulter, liberals have long vilified Senator Joseph McCarthy as part of a conspiracy to conceal the supposed truth that Democratic administrations, starting with FDR, were rife with Soviet spies. Rather than admit that one of the greatest U.S. presidents of all time was hoodwinked by America's new nuclear-age enemy, the Soviet Union, Democrats instead turned Joseph McCarthy into a grand symbol of everything un-American. Coulter's goal in *Treason* is not just to rebut claims that President George W. Bush abused Americans' civil liberties and violated the Constitution, but to reframe the entire debate in terms of the habitual tendency of liberals to cover up their track record of working to destroy America. In response to Democrats comparing the hunt for terrorists after 9/11 to McCarthyism, Coulter could now say that the real issue is not terrorism at all, but the liberal tendency to "side with the enemy" and then demonize anyone who dares question their treason.

Coulter's imagined liberal conspiracy surrounding the Alger Hiss affair and the McCarthy Senate testimony sessions may seem esoteric to most readers at first. And yet, the argument leads the reader to forget for a moment that FDR ended the Great Depression, massively strengthened America's infrastructure, defeated global fascism and protected working Americans. Even though the U.S. government did not experience Soviet domination under FDR, Truman or anyone else, Coulter still argues that FDR was ground zero of liberals' treason which, as everyone knows, is a crime punishable by death. Anyone who enters into a debate about terrorism or the occupation of Iraq with Coulter is instantly yanked into the broad logic of treason.

The violence in Coulter's logic about liberal treason flows out of a tactic she repeatedly uses that might best be described as "murder by proximity." The technique begins with Coulter defining an enemy of the United States by reference to the "murders" that the leader of that particular nation or ideology wrought. She then associates prominent political figures in the Democratic Party with the act of murder by mentioning them in the text either right before or right after the word "murder." The effect is subtle, but effective, as in these examples where she associates FDR's name with murders committed by Stalin:

> The principal difference between fifth columnists in the Cold War versus the war on terrorism is that you could sit next to a Communist on a subway without asphyxiating. The second difference is, by the end of World War II, Roosevelt's pal Joseph Stalin had murdered twenty million people.[12]

> On Roosevelt's watch, the Soviets took eastern Poland, Moldavia, Lithuania, Latvia, Estonia, and Albania. "Uncle Joe" murdered an estimated twelve to twenty million people, and forced at least ten million into slave labor.[13]

Or this example where she associates Truman's name with murders committed in Communist China:

> Under President Truman (1945-1953), we lost China, the most populist nation on earth. The Red Chinese occupied Tibet. Over the next four decades Chinese Communists would murder between 34 million and 64 million Chinese and an estimated 1 million Tibetans.[14]

At first reading, it may seem semantic to notice the number of times Coulter's text conjoins the names of Democrats with descriptions of enemies as "murderous," but by the end of the book, there is no doubt that she uses such a strategy. In addition to "murder"—which she mentions on pages 34, 43, 81, 155, 188, 191, 193, 194, 207, and 211 of *Treason*—Coulter also associates Democrats with other words evoking extreme violence, most notably "torture" and "nuclear annihilation." Democrats' supposed affinity for murderous dictators becomes the common thread in Coulter's invented "essence" of American liberalism, thus freeing her from actually having to prove any of her claims. Instead she just unrolls page after page of "just like before" style arguments about liberals continuing to appease murderers. Coulter's arguments about Democrats who supposedly endorsed murder and nuclear annihilation by America's enemies gives *Treason* a doomsday quality to it. If a reader somehow came to the book with no prior knowledge of American history or politics or current events, they might easily conclude that the United States had been destroyed many times over as a result of an endless string of treasonous conspiracies by Democrats. If a reader did have a general familiarity with American history, but was persuaded by Coulter's logic, one would think that liberals who critique the war on terror might in fact be leftover Communist sympathizers, or worse, covert Soviet spies still carrying out their missions. Often, for example, when I post an article about the U.S. occupation of Iraq on a public web site or on *Frameshop*, a conservative reader will accuse me of being a communist. It was not until I read Coulter's *Treason* that I understood why. The fact that I neither write nor speak about communism any more than any other public intellectual is not the issue. What makes me a communist, supposedly, is that I dare to argue against the policies of President Bush. Exactly like the liberals who, according to Coulter, created the negative myth about McCarthy and who cavorted with murderous foreign heads of state, my critiques are just the latest treason "intrinsic to" the entire liberal "worldview."[15]

The issue pushed aside by Coulter's violent language about liberals is "service." The debate is about a creative democracy that encourages civic participation, instead of a corrupt system that ruins the lives of citizens who step into the arena of public life.

The violent language in Coulter's written and spoken words are the ultimate political anesthesia, to borrow Orwell's phrase. And as Coulter often repeats, she makes a lot of money doing it. Few people in broadcast media claim to respect or admire Coulter, but they can't seem to resist inviting her back time and time again onto their shows—whereupon she never fails to produce a sexually graphic, physically threatening or just plain violent accusation against liberals and their supposed relentless quest to destroy America. The same is true of her writing:

> In the war on terrorism, liberals once again are cheering for the destruction of civil society.[16]

Coulter sells books and TV marketing departments sell advertising. Everyone wins, except the readers and viewers.

John Dewey wrote in 1939 that the challenges America faced in his day were much more complicated than the challenges faced by the founders of the republic, and that the ability to handle them successfully demanded an extraordinary level of creativity and inventiveness. "It is a challenge," Dewey wrote, "to do for the critical and complex conditions of today what the men of earlier days did for far simpler conditions."[17] That insight led Dewey to place great value in an American public sphere built to enable and sustain the capacity for democratic creativity. What made that inventiveness possible was not the emergence of a talented few, but widespread participation in the process of forming public opinion. Dewey's idea of creative democracy is one of the foundations of the American system of education and one of the core principles that has helped to sustain this country through even the most difficult of times. Americans often talk about "We the People" as a core value on which the nation was established. Creative democracy is a working principle that takes the abstract notion of "We the People" and gives concrete direction for individuals to do the pragmatic work of civic life. Coulter's rhetoric not only obscures this process, it poisons the soil in which civic identity takes root. Dewey himself commented on the dangers that fear-inducing rhetoric could pose to the creative pragmatism of American democracy:

> Merely legal guarantees of civil liberties of free belief, free expression, free assembly are of little avail if in daily freedom of communication, the give and take of ideas, facts, experiences, is choked by mutual suspicion, by abuse, by fear and hatred. These things destroy the essential condition of the democratic way of living even more effectually than open coercion.[18]

Coulter's rhetoric is precisely that danger that Dewey foresaw. Dewey likens the condition of the democratic way of living to breathable air, and constant abuse to fumes. It is a resonant metaphor. Yet, in today's political environment, the image of fumes is too subtle to adequately describe the impact of broadcast media. Radiation is probably a better metaphor. How then can Americans restore the conditions of a democratic way of life? The answer lies in the deceptively simple, yet fundamentally democratic idea of service.

In the American system, we typically divide "service" into two distinct channels: military and civilian. It was not always this way. In a speech delivered on October 5, 1960, then Senator John F. Kennedy proposed to tap into America's youthful idealism by affixing the language of military organization to a variety of civilian programs that would be conceived alongside of military enlistment as "service in the national interest."[19] Although he saw the logic in Kennedy's distinction between military and civilian service, his opponent for the presidency, Richard Nixon insisted that Kennedy's argument was neither an appeal to American idealism nor an attempt to cultivate the conditions in which creative democracy could thrive. To Nixon, Kennedy's proposal for a youth conservation corps at home and a Peace Corps abroad was nothing more than a political tactic to earn the votes of draft dodgers. Nixon argued that Kennedy's proposal was tantamount to an "escape hatch" for those seeking to avoid service in the Armed Forces and would ultimately destroy the entire system.[20] The Peace Corps did not, of course, weaken or undermine anything, but instead became the very system by which Americans were able to dedicate their lives to cultivating creative democracy abroad.

A concern for cultivating the conditions of creative democracy returned in the various campaign proposals of many of the 2008 Democratic presidential candidates. John Edwards proposed widespread volunteer service with the goal of tapping into youth idealism in order to staff projects that would diminish or even end poverty in America. Chris Dodd proposed a reworked Peace Corp style service program that would have sent young people abroad to help cultivate the conditions of democracy overseas, and then contribute their experiences to creative democracy at home. Barack Obama proposed integrating volunteer service directly into America's educational system. Hilary Clinton proposed the creation of a U.S. Public Service Academy with the goal of cultivating civilian leaders responsible for maintaining creative democracy. Each of the plans to revive the American service tradition proposal, in its own way, not only cheered for the cultivation of civil society, but would set in motion specific steps for tilling that soil. Cynicism towards American democracy, in other words, must be opposed by participation in the deliberative discussion, not simply by comity.

Deliberative discussion has been drowned out by violent pundit rhetoric, but it is still the most important and most distinctive aspect of American democracy. In its classic form, deliberative discussion was conceived by the framers of the Constitution—Jefferson in particular—as an ongoing series of conversations amongst local groups of farmers who would, by gathering together at regular intervals, learn from each other what was needed in order to make the best decisions.[21] In this respect, early ideas of deliberative democracy were rooted in the act of linking local information to individual conduct for the benefit of the common welfare. What did citizens need to know about the realities of their immediate worlds in order to make the best decisions? Pragmatism was the bottom line. Today, the deliberative conversation is no longer led by local groups of farmers, but by a wide array of citizens, the majority of whom, instead of gathering together, now spend far more time tuning in to the media. Where local information once dominated America's deliberative debate, broadcast media now turns far-away events into issues of concern. Unfortunately, the flood of media information does not strengthen the powers of observation and deliberation, but instead tends to "stimulate emotion and…leave behind a deposit of opinion," as Dewey once observed.[22] While the 24-hour news cycle has created new opportunities for Americans to follow global events, it has all but covered up what remains of our pragmatic tradition of civic debate based in the observation of actual events.

The debate about "service" in American politics, thus, touches on new ways to cultivate citizens that can make skilled use of all the information they encounter. The key is not simply to dismiss broadcast media as detrimental to healthy democracy, but to find ways to balance information from direct observation with information delivered by TV, radio and the Internet. The goal is not to limit the flow of facts, but to find the best way for citizens to make informed decisions about their own conduct, as well as the conduct of the country. It is a tall order, and an ideal never quite reached, but pursuit of it should and could occupy much more of our time.

To revive and maintain a healthy deliberative democracy, Americans must reconsider the value of those arenas where ideas and information are exchanged for the purpose of making better-reasoned decisions. But we must also be willing to imagine ourselves individually and collectively not simply as listeners offering opinions in a world dominated by media, but as participants who frequent new places and forums for discussion, with Jefferson's vision of face-to-face interaction and the current global media reality in mind. In many ways, the generation referred to as the "Millennials" (those born post-1980) is already involved with this task, creating and inhabiting these new forums with regularity and enthusiasm. The result is a sudden and unexpected catching up for American politicians and media alike. Whereas past generations differentiated themselves culturally through alternative forms of entertainment or dress, the Millennials distinguish themselves by their ability to master technology that enables them to use the flow of information in a way that the Baby Boomers (1946-1964) and Generation X (1965-1979) cannot. And there is increasing interest among Millennials in being more than consumers of that information for personal advantage. Thus, a conversation has begun, complete with policy discussions, about harnessing online social networking technology for the practice of government itself. It is an amazing discussion and we are just at the beginning.

Service, however, remains the key concept underlying these innovations in our deliberative democracy—the idea of stepping into the civic arena to work for achievements that benefit something much larger than oneself. In that environment, we must be willing to overcome the tendency to greet acts of service with accusations and character smears, a tendency embodied by the mocking, violent rhetoric of Ann Coulter. Inevitably, our system of media-infused politics will push in the direction of productive deliberation for collective gain to compete against, if not displace, the current situation.

5. THE BILLY CLUB

On April 5, 2007, television and radio host Bill O'Reilly engaged Geraldo Rivera in an on-air conversation about the recent deaths of two Virginia Beach high school teenagers. Several days earlier, while driving with a blood alcohol level well above the legal limit, Alfredo Ramos had crashed head on into a car driven by 17-year old Alison Kunhardt, who subsequently died along with her passenger, 16-year old Tessa Trenchant. Ramos was subsequently charged with involuntary aggravated manslaughter. The case quickly turned into a media firestorm after two facts about Ramos emerged: one, he had been arrested for drunk driving several months before; and two, he had been charged not only with DUI in that earlier arrest, but also for driving without a valid driver's license, having been caught with a so-called "Mexican ID," instead of a Virginia state license. Ramos, in other words, had immigrated to the United States without a visa, thereby making him an "illegal."

O'Reilly and Rivera argued the case in an exchange filled with violent verbal abuse. While O'Reilly did not actually strike Geraldo, it seemed quite possible that he was going to at this moment in the segment:

RIVERA: It could be a Jewish drunk. It could be a Polish

drunk.

O'REILLY: But this guy didn't have to be here.

RIVERA: It could be an Irish drunk.

O'REILLY: No.

RIVERA: It could be an Italian drunk. What the hell difference does it make?

O'REILLY: It makes plenty of difference!

RIVERA: It does not, Bill.

O'REILLY: He doesn't have a right to be here!

RIVERA: He didn't commit a felony.

O'REILLY: He doesn't have a right to be in this country!

RIVERA: What–but that has nothing to do with the fact that he was a drunk!

O'REILLY: Yes, it does! He should have been deported! He should have been deported! And this mayor and the police chief didn't deport him![1]

In this case, the exclamation points in the transcript indicate moments where O'Reilly barked loudly and jabbed his finger towards Rivera's face. In fact, a video clip of O'Reilly shouting and jabbing his finger at a stunned Rivera circulated on the Internet and was discussed on political talk shows for the next week. Days after the O'Reilly show incident, nobody except the parents and friends of Alison Kunhardt and Tessa Trenchant remembered their names, nor the name of the man whose careless abuse of alcohol had resulted in their tragic deaths, Alfredo Ramos. Instead, O'Reilly's tirade against Geraldo became the story.

The outburst in his exchange with Rivera offered a window onto the disturbing mix that defines O'Reilly's on-screen persona. In a medium defined by talk, O'Reilly thrives on heated confrontation that he promotes as an antidote to media and political spin. When not yelling or jabbing fingers at guests whose perspectives diverge from his own, O'Reilly berates them with his signature crankiness. And it is hard to deny that this confrontational style—coupled with a relentless self-promotion—accounts in large part for his popularity. In an earlier encounter with author and radio host—and current Senatorial candidate—Al Franken during the 2003 *Los Angeles Times* Book Fair, O'Reilly demonstrated with even greater clarity how he strategically straddles the line between talk and the threat of physical violence. Franken criticized O'Reilly for, among other things, what he saw as O'Reilly's false claims about winning two highly prestigious Peabody Awards for journalism, a criticism that Franken had also included in his book *Lies and the Lying Liars Who Tell Them: A Fair and Balanced Look At The Right.*[2] When Franken finished speaking, O'Reilly changed the tone with this sharp exchange:

> O'REILLY: We're supposed to be on here for 15 minutes. This idiot goes 35, OK? All he's got in 6 1/2 years is that I misspoke, that I labeled a Polk Award a Peabody. He writes it in his book. He tries to make me out to be a liar.
> AL FRANKEN, COMEDIAN: No, no, no, no.
> O'REILLY: Hey, shut up.
> FRANKEN: No, you shut up.
> O'REILLY: You had your 35 minutes. Shut up.[3]

What the transcript does not quite relay is the threat in O'Reilly's voice. The video recording of O'Reilly telling Franken to shut up did relay that sense, which was the main reason it circulated the Internet so widely in the days following the confrontation.[4] Just as O'Reilly's yelling and jabbing startled viewers who were watching his on-air conversation with Geraldo Rivera, O'Reilly's barking "shut up" at Franken struck many viewers as a school-yard taunt by someone with anger control issues instead of the behavior of a journalist. In fact, no other widely-viewed television host routinely uses his voice and his body to break the rules of civil exchange quite the way O'Reilly does. The effect is to blur the line between debate and physical confrontation, thereby raising the specter that the battle of ideas will devolve into an exchange of blows. During the exchange with Rivera, for example, while O'Reilly did not physically assault Geraldo, his tone and demeanor suggested that the rule separating verbal and physical confrontation had been inexplicably suspended.

In O'Reilly's descriptions of himself, particularly in his book *Culture Warrior*, his signature belligerence is not seen as a breach of decorum but as a necessary tactic in his chosen role as media and political muckraker. Although O'Reilly never admits that he believes violent rhetoric is a crucial part of good journalism, he defines his broadcast persona and mission as a pundit through an extended metaphor of war, likening himself to a warrior waging battle against a dangerous enemy that he claims threatens America. For O'Reilly, the dangerous enemy is liberal journalists, thinkers and politicians. Beyond the lens of war, O'Reilly likens himself to a street fighter unafraid to duke it out with media and political figures whose views diverge from his own. Leveraging this idea of himself as a journalist boxer, O'Reilly re-imagines political debate as a bare-knuckle brawl, whereas most journalists approach it as an exchange of ideas. These paired concepts of war and boxing define how O'Reilly proudly defines himself in his writing, and in the way he uses his broadcast to influence civic debate. Physically imposing and one of the most well-known television personalities in America, O'Reilly talks about himself and approaches every show as if he is a scrappy underdog confronting dangerous bullies—those bullies being writers and politicians.

O'Reilly published *Culture Warrior* in 2006 and it went on to rapidly become a "megabestseller," which is the word he uses to describe the sales of his previous books *The O'Reilly Factor*, *The No Spin Zone*, and *Who's Looking Out For You*. Perhaps the most remarkable aspect of O'Reilly's work, which comes across more clearly in his writing than during his TV show, is the extent to which Bill O'Reilly is the central subject that interests Bill O'Reilly. Although *Culture Warrior* can be described as a conservative pundit's take on the state of American journalism and politics, it is more memoir than manifesto, more self-mythology than program for action. O'Reilly has a gift for turning his own experiences into narratives that depict him in epic proportions, casting himself as the lonely hero of the modern age, threatened by armies of the night:

> Whenever I've witnessed strife, I've met far more villains than heroes, but both are relatively rare. Most human beings are neither heroes nor villains but decent people who choose to sit things out until pushed beyond a reasonable limit. For a variety of reasons that I will explain, I have chosen to jump into the fray.[5]

From the first page of *Culture Warrior* through to the last, O'Reilly is unapologetically self-aggrandizing. There are few heroes in the world, but his book is the story of one of them: Bill O'Reilly.

Throughout the book, O'Reilly follows an extended war metaphor to describe his work as a TV host who has made on-air confrontation with guests his signature motif. Keywords invoking a military scenario pepper the text with unsubtle regularity. America is in the midst of a "vicious culture war," he explains. "And war is exactly the right term." What follows is O'Reilly's predictable recasting of civic debate into violent conflict through the use of such terms as "battlefields," "forces," and "enemies." While most who know his work would describe him as a right-wing broadcaster, O'Reilly fashions himself a crusader against neither right nor left, but against establishment forces. The battle O'Reilly fights, in his view, is not against the ideological divide, but one much broader and basic. It is the war of the righteous against the powerful. He unfolds this vision of himself as the anti-establishment crusader by explaining the original purpose behind his show *The O'Reilly Factor*:

> The Factor concept is very simple: Watch all those in power, including and especially the media, so they don't injure or exploit the folks, everyday Americans. Never before in the

United Stats had a television news guy dared to criticize other journalists on a regular basis. The late Peter Jennings, a friend, told me I was crazy to do it. "These people will not allow anyone to scrutinize them," he said. "They will come after you with a vengeance." And so they have.[6]

The villain, however, has a logic that extends beyond control of the airwaves and injurious threats to "the folks" as O'Reilly often refers to the American public. Consequently, O'Reilly as crusader is more than just "a television news guy"; he is the anti-establishment hero, with an army of "traditionalists" on the right and "secular progressives" on the left. In this imagined battle, O'Reilly portrays himself as fighting against the "secular-progressive" shock troops as part of a thankless effort to save America.

Giving the enemy forces a name and a face, O'Reilly lays out the stakes of the battle in a futuristic chapter called "The Conflict: America in the Year 2020?" in which he presents the imaginary transcript of a State of the Union speech delivered by "President of the United States, Gloria Hernandez." Win the war, he tells his readers, or soon the S-P shock troops will see to it that a Latino rules over us—and a woman, no less. President Hernandez describes with pride a straw-man vision of multiculturalism-cum-communism, where religion is all but banned, wealth is redistributed by the government, and politicians brag about ridding the country of greed and bias. "The new world order has indeed arrived," states President Hernandez triumphantly. "And I am proud to be the one to lead America into the promised land of collective prosperity."[7] She embodies perfectly the misguided and half-century out-of-date stereotype of the American liberal who dreams of creating a repressive socialist future. The result in O'Reilly's hands is less a totalitarian nightmare than a goofy attempt at Orwellian shtick.

The battle to stave off the Latinas-on-top nightmare of a Secular-Progressive future leads us to O'Reilly's glibly sexist and bigoted vision of President Hernandez. She is the driving force behind

O'Reilly's vision of the future, where progressive "fanatics" wage "political jihad" against the traditionalists.[8] Flanked by Hollywood fanatics, the American Civil Liberties Union leads the progressive army. O'Reilly brands the ACLU a "fascist organization" because "they seek to impose their worldview on America...by gaming the legal system" instead of by popular vote.[9] Having equated the ACLU with genocidal political movements of the twentieth century, O'Reilly then identifies the enemy generals. Chief among them is the "shadowy" George Lakoff, a cognitive linguist dubbed by O'Reilly the "Secular-Progressive Jedi master." According to O'Reilly, Lakoff seeks to establish a socialist regime in America via analysis of American political language that is, supposedly, "standard-issue communist thought."[10] The ACLU is a fascist organization, while Lakoff is a communist "God."[11]

O'Reilly reserves even more derision for philanthropists with an interest in progressive issues, targeting George Soros in particular, whom he accuses of undermining American efforts to defend itself from terrorist attack. Soros also supposedly funded a secular progressive "terrorist enabler," Lynne Stewart, who was prosecuted under the new laws passed by the Bush administration for helping Sheikh Omar Abdel-Rahman, the blind religious leader jailed for inciting his followers to truck-bomb the World Trade Center in 1993. Because Soros' provided financial assistance to Stewart during her trial, O'Reilly paints him as a man who nonchalantly helps terrorists.[12] In O'Reilly's vision of the culture war, Soros is the ominous power behind the progressive threat. As powerful as they are, however, it is difficult to take the fight to men like Soros because they remain in the shadows and largely off the public stage. The real culture war O'Reilly chooses to fight, therefore, is a battle to control broadcast media.

O'Reilly sees successful journalism as being about confrontation. Watching *The O'Reilly Factor*, you can discern a sense of discomfort in the faces of those who appear on the show. Both liberals and conservatives are set on edge by O'Reilly's style of speech and his tendency to treat civic debate as combat. Likewise, reading *Culture Warrior* leaves one feeling that O'Reilly's strategy as a writer is to get under the skin of his reader—to write with a sneer. Moreover, O'Reilly constantly pushes two claims about himself: (1) that he is a financial and professional success, and (2) that he is a victim. His tendency to push both of these claims to the extreme seems at first to be the rhetorical tactic of a media provocateur. Yet, the extremism gives his writing and speaking a palpable sense of intellectual insecurity. O'Reilly writes and speaks with the studied sarcasm of someone who wants to be seen as a purveyor of street-corner common sense. Whereas other TV anchors push the elevated diction of a refined professional, O'Reilly talks with the staccato voice of a "wise-guy." "C'mon…" he often says to guests on his show to cut them off. "Nice," he writes, when disagreeing. While none of these approaches to speaking are problematic by themselves, they become so when O'Reilly claims to be using them to bring about truth and justice. In reality, his tactics are designed to get a reaction from viewers who delight in the unease of O'Reilly's guests.

O'Reilly's obsession with confrontation leads him to recast most political issues he takes on in almost absurdist hyperbole. In the summer of 2007, for example, during a prolonged effort to confront liberal bloggers, O'Reilly claimed multiple times that the website *Daily Kos* was "nothing different than the Nazi Party or the Ku Klux Klan."[13] At first, it seemed silly to hear O'Reilly compare a liberal website known for colorful discussions of contemporary politics to an American organization infamous for lynching African-Americans and a German political movement notorious for perpetrating industrialized genocide against European Jewry. The end result is maddening, however, as O'Reilly combines these statements—and many more like them—with a steely refusal to admit error on any issue. Instead, of apologizing, O'Reilly views any dissent from his hyperbolic accusations as evidence of those dissenters' collusion with a system conspiring against the little guy. O'Reilly has the uncanny ability to cut off the exchange of ideas through confrontation, physical intimidation and, when necessary, tilting into the absurd. The result is a media figure whose antics do not just distract public discussion of key issues, but trip up attempts at civic debate itself.

The ever-present threat of physical confrontation that O'Reilly injects into his TV persona is not a symbolic subtext teased out by critics, but a badge of honor that O'Reilly himself uses as way of grounding himself in an ethnic and geographic lineage. In the opening section of *Culture Warrior*, O'Reilly invites his reader to see his combative nature as patrimony inherited from his immigrant ancestors:

> Maybe it helps that many of my Irish ancestors were warriors. They lived in County Cavan and fought Oliver Cromwell when he devastated Ireland in the name of the British Commonwealth. They lost that fight. Later, some of them emigrated to America during the great famine of the 1840s. More came later. My paternal grandfather fought in World War I, then became a New York City police officer. He was one tough SOB. I have his billy club in my desk drawer. It was well used. Come to think of it, maybe I was named after that club.[14]

O'Reilly continues on to describe how the Great Depression crippled his father with fear, thereby temporarily derailing the transmission of the warrior spirit through the generations. Reflecting on the financial difficulty his own father experienced, O'Reilly recalls making a personal vow never to allow the system or "any individual" to push him around. O'Reilly the combative and physically threatening media personality reinvents himself as the legacy of an ethnic fighting spirit which was temporarily driven underground in the pervious generation and was then reborn in the guise of a TV man without fear.

Standing on the shoulders of the giants of County Cavan, O'Reilly transformed his grandfather's billy club into an endless battle against the enemy, which he defines as just about any TV broadcaster who does not work for FOX. Dan Rather, Peter Jennings, Katie Couric, Tom Brokaw, Ted Koppel, Walter Cronkite, Bill Moyers, Lou Dobbs, even Jay Leno are all "S-P" enemy agents to varying degree. John Stossel, Monica Crowley, Joe Scarborough and Regis Philbin are the only non-FOX folks to make O'Reilly's short list of "traditionalist" broadcasters. Once constructed, O'Reilly's tale of the Irish warrior surrounded by hostile enemies is intended to provide his reader with an objective correlative sufficient for them to recognize that his perpetual angry belligerence is not a personality disorder or a ratings gimmick, but an outward manifestation of an inner struggle against seemingly insurmountable injustice. Lesser men have collapsed under the weight of it. O'Reilly rises each day and fights the war.

After defining most everyone from the outset as an enemy, it becomes hard to distinguish levels of threat in O'Reilly's culture war. Who are the most dangerous secular progressive enemies and how are readers to understand this? The answer for O'Reilly is to illustrate the danger of contemporary threats by comparing them to what he sees as similar dangers in the past. For example, after castigating the ACLU as a "fascist organization" in the opening of *Culture Warrior*, midway through the book he qualifies that claim by comparing them to another well-known enemy group:

> Who do you think Osama bin Laden supports in the American culture war: the traditionalists or the secular-progressives? Not so fast…if Osama was calling the shots in the United States, the ACLU would be, in theory, very, very busy. In reality, they'd be dead. But think about what I am about to put forth: From his hideout somewhere in the Muslim world, Osama bin Laden and his cohorts have got to be cheering on the S-P movement, because its most

fanatical adherents are opposed to the bedrock strengths of traditional America.[15]

O'Reilly states clearly that al Qaeda and the secular progressive movement are at odds politically, but the comparison is marshaled to argue that both groups share a common end even if they are divided by ideology, practice, and geography. The point is that both organizations stand against traditional America, as O'Reilly views it. Furthermore, because the ACLU has advocated fair legal representation even for terrorists caught within the United States, O'Reilly classifies them as enemies working on the cultural front to advance the same goal of destroying America as terrorists working on the military front. Thus, O'Reilly's reader is led to understand that the ACLU is the cultural wing of a violent plot to overthrow America, and that al Qaeda is the violent wing of a cultural plot to ensure the same destruction. Either way they define each other by their supposed mutual goals as extreme enemies. Even worse, the ACLU, according to O'Reilly, actively works to undermine efforts by traditionalists to protect the country from violence, which they accomplish by "creating a fog that damages our counterterrorism effort." As so many right-wing pundits do at this point in their argument, O'Reilly plays the ace up his sleeve to drive home his point:

> Don't these people get 9/11? Doesn't the S-P movement understand the danger America faces from terrorist fanatics who would use nuclear weapons, should they acquire them, against us?[16]

The question is rhetorical, as O'Reilly has already damned the secular progressive enemy as having the same goal of destroying America as terrorists by arguing that both ideologies share the "true believer" and "fanatic" conviction that America is "a bad place" or "an evil country." O'Reilly claims this supposed fanatical anti-Americanism as the key to understanding the entire secular progressive movement.[17] His exaggerated and sarcastic claims are attempts to redefine political debate as a mortal threat to the life of the country, reducing critiques of Republican leadership to a menacing, formulaic logic where debate about foreign policy decisions somehow results in grave danger. His likening of bin Laden to the ACLU clarifies little. Instead it scuttles the debate by inviting readers and viewers to see opposition politics as domestic handmaidens to foreign terrorists. Ironically, O'Reilly characterizes one of the high points in American political debate, the moment immediately following 9/11 when Americans felt free to debate what caused the growth of Islamic extremist networks trained in guerilla-style terrorist tactics, as evidence of enemy penetration into media and politics. Specifically, a small number of left-wing intellectuals and activists presented their views that past American foreign policy bore responsibility for originating this global phenomenon as a result of efforts to leverage the mujahideen in Afghanistan against the Soviets in the 1980s. While this is a well-known fact, O'Reilly argues that speaking of it after 9/11 was tantamount to treason and evidence that secular progressives were apologists for al Qaeda.

Ultimately, O'Reilly's foray into political debate after 9/11 defined the secular progressive enemy as a danger to America on par with al Qaeda. To O'Reilly, progressive leadership embodied a form of military appeasement that had been dormant since the days when Chamberlain appeased Hitler. As such, O'Reilly sees liberalism as a return to the mindset that appeased the Nazis. History has come full circle, O'Reilly argues in *Culture Warrior,* and men of principle have been called to see to it that the gains of western civilization do not slip back to the days of pre-World War II weakness. Hitler is the archetypal enemy abroad, but it is specter of Chamberlain's desire to placate evil that must stir us to the fight at home.

In some cases liberals do more than just appease tyranny the way Chamberlain appeased Hitler—they act like Hitler, too. O'Reilly recounts an incident where a court threw out a conviction based on a mother's testimony against a child. He cites this case as evidence that the ACLU's advocacy on behalf of underage criminal offenders mimics techniques used by Hitler:

> This is a strategy—mentally separate children from their parents—that has been practiced by totalitarian govern-ments throughout history. In Nazi Germany, there was the Hitler Youth. Chairman Mao created the Children's Corps in Red China. Stalin and Castro rewarded children who spied on their parents. That's the blueprint. If you want to change a country's culture and traditions, children must first abandon them and embrace a new vision. Hello, secu-lar-progressivism in the USA. I'm not saying these people are little Adolfs; I am saying that they have adopted some totalitarian tactics in their strategies.[18]

"I am not saying" they are Nazis, he assures his readers. He goes on, however, to say that secular progressives use the same techniques that the Nazis used to turn children against their parents in order to create the core ideological base of a movement that will rise up to destroy the country, put dissenters in concentration camps, and promote utopian visions doomed to collapse into genocide.

Underneath this linking of S-P thinkers and organizations to Hitler, Mao, Stalin, and Castro is a calculated attempt to undermine any debate about foreign policy, law, or economics by shouting about history's most horrific cases of mass violence. The names of infamous totalitarian dictators are not just invoked, in other words, to demon-ize leftist organizations, journalists and activists, but to transform discussions of policies into emotional fist-fights. Having accused his political opposition of using the same techniques as genocidal mass murderers, O'Reilly knows that he has ended the debate, whether the subjects are the causes of terrorism, the rights of children, or economic policy. O'Reilly's Hitler talk is the equivalent of tossing up a checkerboard, storming out of the room, and then immediately holding a press conference to talk about how your opponent plays unfair. If executed well, nobody will remember what actually happened. It's all the enemy's fault.

The issue overlooked as a result of violent language on right-wing talks shows is "protection." The debate is about building a society that limits cruelty and danger, as opposed to a country that sows resentment and hostility.

O'Reilly's book *Culture Warrior* reveals what is often difficult to see during the violent confrontational broadcasts of *The O'Reilly Factor*. His on-screen rhetoric emerges from his broad conception that civic debate is a war and that he is not just a warrior but the resurrection of a great genealogy of warriors. Once inside this warrior world, O'Reilly uses physical confrontation and violent rhetorical outbursts in defense of those he claims are the victims of a fascist and covert league of media figures and politicians. These fascist figures and politicians abuse their power and work in concert with the goals and objectives of the most murderous enemies America has ever faced, driving the nation to the brink of self-destruction. This war is not merely of convenience or of words, but of American survival. If it ruffles a few feathers or makes a few enemy soldiers wriggle in their underground lairs, then that is how it must be.

The problem with this tale of war and suffering that O'Reilly spins is that in order to claim that one is a victim, one also needs to show some kind of suffering at the hand of the so-called enemy. Unfortunately for O'Reilly, the only suffering he identifies comes in the form of his disagreement with liberals on political issues. O'Reilly never suffers himself. He fights for others. At least, that is his claim. The disruption that O'Reilly forces into an issue, however, rarely has anything to do with the issue itself. Ultimately, whenever he steps in to wage war on behalf of some imagined traditionalist victim of secular progressive treachery, O'Reilly ends up creating a controversy about himself and little else. How can we move past his disruptive way of recasting cultural and civic debate?

Curiously, the answer is in the text of *Culture Warrior* itself, in an off-hand remark where O'Reilly lashes out at liberals who participate in open-format Internet political forums:

> If you really want to see just how "caring" and humane the secular-progressive movement is, visit some of their black-hearted Web sites. If the hatred and libel you see are examples of S-P caring, somewhere the Marquis de Sade is cheering.[19]

According to O'Reilly, the writings on liberal blogs are on par with the eighteenth century French aristocrat infamous for his enjoyment of making others suffer for no reason other than his own entertainment, and after whom the word "sadism" was coined. Liberal blogs, of course, have nothing in common with the Marquis de Sade, but O'Reilly's false comparison, ironically, shines a light on the overuse of sadistic rhetoric by right-wing political pundits.

American philosopher Richard Rorty argued that the purpose of politics is not to advance or defend a single, all-encompassing truth—be it traditionalist, progressivism or otherwise—but to bind people together in opposition to cruelty and humiliation. According to Rorty, since the 1960s, the American left has been successful not at controlling vast sections of American media or politics, but at lowering the level of casual humiliation and cruelty that Americans visit upon each other. Speaking of the influence over several decades of new academic programs that teach students to value cultural difference, Rorty observed:

> Especially among college graduates, the casual infliction of humiliation is much less socially acceptable than it was during the first two-thirds of the century. The tone in which educated men talk about women, and educated whites about blacks, is very different from what it was before the Sixties. Life for homosexual Americans, beleaguered and danger-

ous as it still is, is better than it was before Stonewall. The adoption of attitudes which the Right sneers at as "politically correct" has made America a far more civilized society that it was thirty years ago. Except for a few Supreme Court decisions, there has been little change for the better in our country's laws since the Sixties. But the change in the way we treat one another has been enormous.[20]

Rorty's insight came before the Bush administration, before the "war on terror," and before *The O'Reilly Factor* all grew to occupy the prominent roles they now hold in America. His description about the improving "tone" in America offers a profound contrast to the shift from the late 1990s to the present day. Whereas Rorty identified a great lowering of "sadism in our society," right-wing pundits since the 1990s have burst forth with a new and violently charged tone that not only advances casual humiliation, but inspires Americans to treat an open society as an opportunity to be sadistic towards each other. What O'Reilly views as a lonely battle to protect the weak from the destructive power of the American left is nothing of the sort. O'Reilly and his cohorts do not protect Americans from suffering, but instead are the bulwark for the return of cruelty via broadcast TV, the second coming of a widespread sadism that Americans worked admirably for a full generation to overcome. Speaking to this problem in the context of an appearance on the *The O'Reilly Factor*, pundit Michael Eric Dyson commented about the disturbing tendency of O'Reilly's viewers to respond to liberals who appear on the show with highly personal, violent verbal threats:

We see [broadcasters talking] on FOX about 'fair and balanced'--when I go on Bill O'Reilly's show—and I tell him this after the show—I get the worst hate mail ever. I get the 'n-word' thrown at me, I get email. And I want Bill O'Reilly to challenge that in public.[21]

Dyson's larger point echoes Rorty's observations about the purpose and promise of politics in America: that it should bind people together in opposition to cruelty. The public square is supposed to be a place that protects American citizens, not a place where they feel threatened or endangered. That Dyson receives "the worst hate mail" following his appearances on FOX suggests that O'Reilly's show fundamentally alters that equation. The result is a radical shift in the tone of civic debate in America, and an increased threat of violence one must endure to participate in it.

O'Reilly is by no means unique in triggering in his viewers the sense that it is not only acceptable but patriotic to confront the political opposition with threats. That is not to suggest that only right-wing pundits in America hurl threats as a substitute for healthy civic disagreement. Once the level of sadism rises in society, the increased cruelty begins to change the behavior of everyone. Nonetheless, while O'Reilly may find comments on open-forum political websites disrespectful, there is no excuse for convincing his viewers that threatening physical harm is an acceptable way to disagree, no matter how much one may oppose the viewpoint that is expressed. In the toxic environment of that new form of interaction, the practical content of political debate suffocates, and only the unproductive exchange of blows survives.

The issue is not one of limiting dissent in the media. We should encourage dissent and protect those who exercise their right to do so. But how that dissent unfolds determines the kind of discussion that follows. Violent language does not have a one-to-one correlation with violent behavior, and to suggest so is misleading. Rather, the content of broadcast speech defines the terms and tenor of a political discussion, and if that content is violent in its expression, theme or logic, then the discussion it sparks tends to be channeled accordingly. Broadcast comedy, melodrama, and conspiracy theory similarly influence discussions and attitudes with their tone in addition to their content. It should come as no surprise, therefore, that

O'Reilly's use of loud, threatening verbal assaults and his well-developed argument about the "S-P" movement as dangerous to the future of the country results in some viewers of *The O'Reilly Factor* speaking out in a similarly threatening tone. Broadcasters can be pugnacious, highly partisan, and promote theories about one side of American culture, but at the same time make an effort to minimize their use of violent language. Speaking back to a majority or minority viewpoint may not always be civil, but it can and should give rise to healthy debate so long as issues have not been overwhelmed by violent language. The risk with violent language is the growth of a political character defined by aggression and, ultimately, authoritarianism.[22]

A less discussed risk than the rise of authoritarianism, however, is the spread of a counterfeit form of muckraking that makes lots of noise, but produces not a lick of public good. "Muckraking" was a name applied to a type of investigative journalism that flourished at the onset of the twentieth century, and which was characterized by a combination of first hand observation, critique of corporate and government excess, and analysis of the underlying factors that led to corruption.[23] The purpose of muckraking was to use the power of the media to push back against corruption that endangered the livelihood and well-being of vast numbers of citizens. Moreover, muckraking journalists often used language that was consciously hard-hitting, a reaction against what was perceived as the flowery, too-soft tone of their peers in mainstream journalism of the time. O'Reilly resurrects the attitude of the muckrakers, but attempts to fit it into a very different task and idiom. Rather than explain how unregulated power endangers the American people, O'Reilly presents a false form of muckraking that actually uses the power of corporate media to attack and undermine debate. The solution is not to silence shows like *The O'Reilly Factor*, but to reclaim a more authentic approach to muckraking journalism with an eye towards diminishing the appeal and value of violent right-wing rhetoric.

Thomas W. Lawson is a classic example of how inspiring muckraking rhetoric can be. Originally a financial advisor and businessman who worked with Standard Oil to establish the powerful Amalgamated Copper Company, in 1905 Lawson wrote *Frenzied Finance*, about the flagrant abuse of law and investor trust by the very company he helped to set up:

> This "System" is a process or a device for the incubation of wealth from the people's savings in the banks, trust, and insurance companies, and the public funds. Through its workings during the last twenty years there has grown up in this country a set of colossal corporations in which unmeasured success and continued immunity from punishment have bred an insolent disregard of law, of common morality, and of public and private right, together with a grim determination to hold on to, at all hazards, the great possessions they have gulped or captured.[24]

Lawson presents a stunning contrast of clarity and purpose to the false muckraking of today's right-wing pundits. *Frenzied Finance* demonstrates that social critique based on first-hand observations is more focused and effective than even the most confrontational violent rhetoric of the contemporary broadcast political media. Lawson understood how to use language in the interest of protecting the public. The power to protect lay in the persuasiveness of clear description. The shock was not the product of staging, but came through the writer's ability to relay the horrific details of corporate behavior to the public. Lawson is only one example of how effective this idiom can be at highlighting the dangers that American citizens face. Other examples include Ida Tarbell writing on Standard Oil, Upton Sinclair writing about the American sausage industry, and more recently, Ralph Nader's work on the dangers citizens faced from automobiles, as well as Barbara Ehrenreich's work on the injustices of minimum wage employment. In each instance, the government took concrete steps to protect the public from the dangers revealed by the muckrakers' writing.

Today, more than ever, the need for journalism to shine a light on the dangers that the "system" poses to American citizens is great. Media has a significant role to play in helping to protect the public, but it cannot do so if it is weighed down by language that diverts attention away from the real dangers.

6. CHRISTMAS KILLERS

On November 28, 2003, Joe Scarborough invited the Reverend Jerry Falwell onto his popular MSNBC show *Scarborough Country.* The topic was a supposed "war" waged by American liberals against the holiday of Christmas. Falwell claimed that the war was fueled by a widespread and growing "hatred for Christ":

SCARBOROUGH: Here to talk about the war on Christmas is William J. Murray. He's the chairman of the Religious Freedom Coalition and the son of the famous atheist Madalyn Murray, who sued to end prayer in school. We also have atheist activist Rob Sherman, the Reverend Jerry Falwell of Liberty University, and Ellen Johnson, an advocate for the separation of church and state. Let me begin with you, Reverend Falwell. Do you believe that Christmas is under attack in America?

FALWELL: Oh, yes, and it has been for a generation. I heard earlier tonight Peggy Noonan talking about how Hollywood hates Ronald Reagan. And, of course, you would add George W. Bush. But the fact is that the hatred for

Christ that exists with groups like the ACLU, Americans United For Separation of Church and State, the Atheist Society, and sometimes the ADL, unfortunately, the hatred for Christ so pales in the hatred for Ronald Reagan. To think that commercial America, retail America, New York or Montgomery, Alabama, it's financial success for the year depends on how well that they do during the celebration of the birth of Christ, and they don't even want to invite him to the party, to me, it is unthinkable.

SCARBOROUGH: Jerry Falwell, what do you say to those on the left and to judges out there who would say it's unconstitutional to have a nativity scene in a town square?

FALWELL: I would say they are a bunch of idiots. It's unreal that, in this country of ours, built on a Judeo-Christian ethic—and, by the way, Islam had nothing to do with the founding of America. But that's another subject. To think that we could not have an Easter celebration or a Christmas celebration, we can sing all the Christmas carols unless they mention Christ—it is—it betrays the hostility, the terrible hostility. I'm for the Star of David. I'm for the menorahs. I'm for Muslim acknowledgment. I'm for any other religious acknowledgement. But I'm against the censorship of Christ from the public square, be it schools, be it Christmas plays, be it 5th Avenue or whatever. I think it is horrendous. And to think that we've allowed it to go this far because a bunch of men and women in robes have arrogantly run away with power that they don't have constitutionally, I think it's obnoxious.[1]

Scarborough's use of the phrase "war on Christmas" did not garner much attention at the time, as few people worried that his use of a violent metaphor to talk about Christmas would lead to any seismic change in the political debate, let alone herald the return of a narrative about non-Christians persecuting Christians during the holiday. Moreover, Christmas 2003 would mark the third full year since George W. Bush had been propelled into office as a result of unprecedented involvement from conservative Christian voters. Thus, many analysts believed Evangelical Christianity had taken up a central and secure place in the American public square.

Prior to John Gibson's 2005 book *The War on Christmas*, Falwell had tried and failed to gain momentum for his war against Christmas in the guise of the "Friend or Foe" campaign launched by the ultra-conservative Liberty Council in 2003. While the difference between "on" and "against" may seem too subtle to be meaningful, Falwell's campaign to "save Christmas" had a distinctly different character than Gibson's book. Whereas Gibson intentionally focused his attention on what he called "secular symbols"—most notably the Christmas tree—Falwell's campaign had a more sacred center, emphasizing what he saw as a secular attack on Christ himself. Falwell's campaign, moreover, was not a media effort involving high-profile talk shows and million-dollar book marketing campaigns, but a grassroots civil rights campaign spearheaded by a team of lawyers from Liberty University and promoted primarily through buttons and bumper stickers. "Friend or Foe" offered a website resource complete with suggested wording for advertising that churches could run in local newspapers and a description of the kind of campaign Falwell was pushing in 2003:

> Liberty Counsel, a nationwide litigation, education, and policy organization dedicated to advancing religious freedom, will bring a lawsuit against any government entity discriminating against religion during this holiday season and will defend any government entity which abides by the Constitution and allows the equal expression of religious views. Liberty Counsel will also defend those who are persecuted for celebrating the religious aspects of Christmas...In essence, we will be a "Friend" to those entities which allow for the constitutionally protected right of

expression but will be a "Foe" of those which attempt to suppress religious liberty.[2]

Falwell saturated "Friend or Foe" with quasi-legalistic phrases that urged followers to see themselves as victims of religious discrimination, and then to draw on the services of the Liberty Counsel to file lawsuits. The campaign also included detailed descriptions explaining how to make sure a Christian display did not violate Supreme Court rulings on secular displays. For example, Falwell suggested including an image of Santa Claus in a public nativity scene.

In terms of style, while the "Friend or Foe" campaign was overtly litigious in its goals, it was not violent in its rhetoric. Instead of using the language of war, Falwell adapted phrasings from traditional Baptist concepts. For example, "Friend or Foe" reworked the Evangelical belief in being "saved" by Christ into proclamations on buttons and bumper stickers that the person bearing the campaign paraphernalia had helped "save" Christmas. In addition, the quirky phrases and bumper sticker phrases were trademarked. Falwell wanted to make sure, apparently, that those secular Americans supposedly discriminating against Christmas could not profit from the Liberty Counsel slogans. Even today, the "Friend or Foe" campaign continues. (Access to the slogans requires a twenty-five dollar donation to the Liberty Counsel.)

Despite the legalistic emphasis in Falwell's campaign, however, right-wing TV pundits immediately began to reframe the "Friend or Foe" language in terms of more militaristic and violent rhetoric. A 2005 on-air discussion between Falwell and John Kasich, former Republican congressman turned FOX News' host, revealed how Falwell's Christmas campaign was reframed in violent terms:

KASICH: In the "religion under siege" segment tonight, we reported earlier this week that some on the religious right, led by the Reverend Jerry Farwell, have mobilized forces to save Christmas from secular factions this season.

One of their first assignments—change Boston Commons holiday tree to a Christmas tree. Reverend Falwell joins us now from Lynchburg, Virginia…All right, Reverend Falwell, you've got this army, like a half a million people who are willing to educate them, litigate. Why do we need to have this army to stand up for Christmas?

FALWELL: Because for whatever reason, there's been a concerted effort to steal Christmas, to deny little children the right to sing "Silent Night," and "Joy to the World" and so forth, while they sing the secular songs which we are very much in favor of. And in Boston, you mentioned the Christmas tree. It was being renamed the holiday tree. To the credit of the mayor of Boston earlier today, he conceded. And he says as long as he is mayor, it will be called the Christmas tree. This is the birthday of Christ. And while we want to honor Muslims, Hindus, Jewish holidays, Christmas should not be victimized by the anti-Christ, anti-religious freedom forces like Americans United and the American Civil Liberties Union.[3]

Kasich recasts Falwell's campaign using an extended war metaphor. Whereas "Friend or Foe" actually talks about discrimination and encourages people to bring legal action, Kasich talks about religion as "under siege" by "secular factions," and Falwell's supporters as an "army." The intent is obvious: transform a somewhat stodgy campaign by a Christian legal advocacy group into a media-driven slap fight. Legal campaigns might be important, in other words, but they do not do much for ratings.

Despite Kasich's violent tweaks of Falwell's story, the Reverend did not pick up on any of the militaristic metaphors in his response. Instead, he talked about denied rights, victimization and freedom of religion. Falwell's answer to Kasich is that Christmas is Christ. Talking about the holiday of Christmas suffering from discrimination is the same as talking about Christ as a victim. Rather than enlisting viewers to see Christmas as a time when secular Americans wage "war," Falwell seemed to want viewers to extend their empathy and dedication to Christ. Kasich's explicit reframing of Falwell, however, was more than just the strategic tweaking of current events that happens in TV production meetings. As a result of Kasich's interview, Falwell's campaign to raise awareness about Liberty Counsel started to pull in more violent themes from early twentieth century versions of the Christmas-as-victim story.

Prior to Falwell, the most famous advocate to save Christmas from abuse was Detroit industrialist Henry Ford. His 1920 book, *The International Jew*, originally published as a series of essays in the *Dearborn Independent*, was Ford's variation on the old conspiracy theory about a cabal of Jews who run the world at the expense of non-Jews. Interestingly, however, the book contains almost fifty references to Christmas, as Ford told a very particular kind of story about how Christmas was attacked and to what end. He did not just say that Jews sought to deny Americans the right to celebrate Christmas, but that Jews sought to encourage non-Jews to silence themselves. In addition, Ford did not emphasize Jewish attacks on Christianity per se, but rather Jewish attacks on the symbolism and celebrations of Christmas in the public forums of the nation. He was not writing about the perfidious medieval Jew who sought to drain Christian babies of their blood and torture the host as if it were Christ, but a shadowy figure who complained about mutual respect and tolerance in order to hoodwink good-hearted Christians into turning against Christmas. Ford repeatedly used violent idioms to make his larger point about a Christian country that was slowly being overrun by a self-serving, hostile and duplicitous minority:

> When Cleveland and Lakewood arranged for a community Christmas, the Cleveland Jewish press said: "The writer of this has no idea how many Jews there are in Lakewood, but if there is only one, there should be no community Christmas, no community religion of any kind." That is not a

counsel of tolerance, it is a counsel of attack. The Christmas literature of American Judaism is fiercer than the flames of the Inquisition. In the month of January, the Jewish press has urged its readers to begin an early campaign against Christmas celebrations the next Christmas—"Only three hundred and sixty days before Christmas. So let us do our Christmas arguing early and take plenty of time to do it."[4]

The key distinction between Falwell's "Friend or Foe" campaign and John Gibson's *The War On Christmas* lay precisely in the way Gibson returned to a way of talking about the attack on secular Christmas that was reminiscent of Ford's. Many readers have and will continue to miss the point of this comparison, but it is vital to make it nonetheless and worth clarifying for emphasis. To say that Gibson's writing is remarkably similar to Ford's is tricky because many critics of Gibson will conclude that his war on Christmas campaign is essentially a new version of an old anti-Semitic canard. To make that conclusion, however, would be a sloppy misreading of Gibson's book—a misreading Gibson pre-empts in the introduction:

> Whose fault is this? Well, for those who like to jump to conclusions, no, it's not just liberal Jews. I should state for the record that my Jewish son helped me to research this book because he agrees that the war on Christmas has gone too far. The large number of foot soldiers waging the war on Christmas is in fact made up mostly of liberal white Christians, some of whom may have Jewish-sounding names (Cohen, Horoschak) that could mislead readers to a dangerous and very unfair conclusion. So let's restate for the record: the wagers of this war on Christmas are a cabal of secularists, so-called humanists, trial lawyers, cultural relativists, and liberal, guilt-wracked Christians—not just Jewish people.[5]

When Gibson writes that it is "not just Jews" waging a war on Christmas, while he may seem disingenuous or cynical, his book is in fact not an anti-Semitic tract. While Ford was wholly consumed by "the Jew" and wrote a book outlining the anti-Semitic theory that Jewish people secretly plan for national and world domination, Gibson fixates on a variation of that devil: the secularist. The "anti-Christmas warriors" are found in organizations historically chock-full of Jewish members, such as the American Civil Liberties Union and Americans for the Separation of Church and State, as well as groups with predominantly Jewish constituents, such as the Anti-Defamation League."[6] However, Gibson also targets Christian organizations, such as the United Church of Christ. In the tradition of Ford, Gibson's weaves a tale of a "conspiracy" to subvert American Christianity, drawing on military metaphors for narrative cohesion.[7]

Gibson's book was the key text that launched the "war on Christmas" into mainstream consciousness. The book itself breaks down into two clear parts. The first portion focuses on regional case studies. Similar to Ford's writing, in each case study Gibson hones in on a single American locale to demonstrate how secular liberals are waging the "war" against Christmas. The seven chapters that make up this part of *The War On Christmas* focus on "secular signs" of the "war," a conscious choice by Gibson to contrast with earlier works on the subject:

> Many Christians still think the nativity scene and the cross should be displayed in public and that fight is continuing. But my book focuses on the instances of very secular signs of Christmas being banned because they are thought to be too Christian or that they would offend someone. Those symbols include Santa Claus, the Christmas tree, the word Christmas, and believe it or not, even the colors red and green.[8]

Most of Gibson's argument hinges on recent Supreme Court rulings defining these contested symbols as non-religious. In case after case, Gibson locates a liberal "secularist" who passed a school or office regulation against the public display of a Christmas symbol on grounds that it evoked religion. Gibson then argues that since the Supreme Court has shown the display in question to be secular and not religious, the only logic behind the liberal campaign is a widespread conspiracy against Christians and Christianity. He defines each of these case studies from Georgia or Oklahoma or Kansas or New Jersey as "battles"[9] or "battlegrounds"[10] or "front lines."[11] In this way, the metaphor of civic debate as a violent war becomes the unifying rhetorical device throughout the book.

Gibson's skill at mixing violent rhetoric and humor is one of the most challenging aspects of *The War on Christmas*. While it may seem odd to suggest that Gibson's book about war against Christians in America rests on a foundation of dry humor, the combination of violence and humor is actually quite common amongst right-wing pundits. While many of the more popular right-wing voices on television and radio use a stylized anger or aggression to appeal to their audience, Gibson's approach has always been irony. In this way, he is the last of an all-but-extinct breed of right-wing pundit activists who used humor as a strategy to undermine a perceived liberal elite hypocrisy on the issue of cultural diversity. Rather than critiquing or confronting advocates for multiculturalism, the right-wing satirist pointed out moments where the advocate for diversity did or said something that might be construed as "intolerant," and then used those moments to supposedly reveal the hypocrisy of the entire movement for multiculturalism. The end result of this satirical approach was a broad belittling of multiculturalism as little more than discrimination against a majority.

Gibson is expert in using humor in this way. In one passage, for example, he uses humor to recount a controversial decision by some public offices in Eugene, Oregon to require that holiday displays in public spaces be non-denominational:

A remarkable process was beginning in the diversity corridors of the city of Eugene: the targeting of Christmas and Christians by the city government under the banner of diversity. But in its very bluntness this policy of anti-Christian bias was unique. Certainly if it were the same bias at work with another group, the policy and the thinking that went into it would be immediately denounced, most loudly perhaps by these very members of the diversity committees. "We started to realize that there was a certain segment of our employees that really felt a little put out by having to deal with Christmas trees. Because it wasn't a part of their culture...'What is this? Is this a Christian organization?'" Couldn't have that.[12]

There was not, of course, any such "targeting of Christmas and Christians by the city government." Gibson casts the public debates about diversity in Eugene as the language of violent repression. The exaggeration, however, has a specific purpose: to set up the straw man example of the city worker tripping over their own intolerance for Christianity under the guise of wanting to defend diversity. After giving the city employees plenty of room to get tangled up in their own words, Gibson undercuts them with a deadpan one-liner: heaven forbid a concern for diversity also be a concern for Christianity.

Gibson's use of humor is seductive. As a rhetorical strategy, humor draws readers into the false story he is telling about an active campaign to exclude Christians from public life in this country. What should be funny to readers is that Gibson made his claim about the exclusion of Christians from public life at the exact moment in American history when Christians were most visible and influential in American public life. In fact, there should be public debate about the place of religious and holiday symbolism in public spaces. These debates are healthy for our democracy and lead, ultimately, to a greater understanding of the relationship between religion, law, and the public square in America. In Gibson's hands, however, these debates indicate no such public debate, but are instead evidence of a conspiracy by secularists to rid America of Christmas, Christianity, and Christians.

Curiously, Gibson's use of irony extends to decidedly unfunny moments—situations where conservatives are confronted with threats of actual violence by those involved in the Christmas decoration controversy. In one section of *The War on Christmas,* Gibson recounts an incident involving Anthony Tarr, Dean of Indiana University School of Law, during a 2002 controversy about Christmas decorations. The story about Indiana is virtually identical to every other example in Gibson's book. In each case, a liberal who believes he or she is valuing diversity by responding to complaints about Christmas decorations in public spaces is revealed by Gibson as a soldier in the "war" against Christmas. In the case of Dean Tarr, however, the situation turned from metaphorical threat to actual danger:

> Tony Tarr wasn't prepared for all that came his way. "Well, you should know that we received death threats about this," he said in an interview with me. "Indeed, I arrived home one evening. And my wife, who is absolutely no shrinking violet, was on the telephone. And it transpired that some religious nut from down in Georgia or somewhere had suggested this notion about her being married to this Antichrist person." Tony Tarr was a practicing Episcopalian and at the moment he was being inundated by e-mail, letters, phone calls, and abuse on the airwaves for perceived bias against Christians and Christmas trees, his house was aglow with miles of Christmas lights, and his special twelve-foot Christmas kangaroo with the red nose was perched on the front yard.[13]

Gibson dwells on the Tarr example not to raise alarm about the death threats he received for questioning the place of Christmas trees in a law school lobby. The detail of the controversy that involved a real threat of violence receives little more than a tongue-in-cheek mention. The problem Gibson dwells on is that Tarr came to Indiana Law School from Australia. As such, Tarr did not understand how the anti-Christmas advocates had appealed to his belief in the value of diversity in order to consciously manipulate him into attacking Christianity. In his comments, Tarr is clearly alarmed at the fact that his wife received phone calls from an out-of-state caller making threats—as would anyone. But for Gibson, the interview quote is used to build a case for Tarr as an unwitting, hapless diversity advocate who should have known what he would get if he started tampering with Christmas trees. The irony is twofold: Tarr perceives himself to be a great promoter of Christmas decorations, having invested so much time and energy into a set of lavish lights for his home, yet is unable to see how the anti-Christmas agents have manipulated him.

Similarly, in a separate episode from Eugene, Oregon, a municipal administrator named Jim Johnson also receives threats following a Christmas decoration controversy. In this instance, while Gibson does not make light of the incident, he again fails to raise any alarm about the violent tone of the reaction to a public policy about holiday decorations. Instead, he focuses on the supposed danger that a municipal employee poses to Christians, Christianity and, most urgently, to Christmas ornaments:

> "In fact, it affected me quite a bit. I was very concerned for my personal safety," Johnson said. "I received a telephone threat, which the police responded to, came up to my house." The difficulty was that while Johnson was receiving vague but ominous threats to himself and his family, he was not there to help protect his family. He was out of town, in

Boston attending a convention of city managers. "So the police officer showed up at my door and talked to my wife about the threat." The police increased the patrols around the Johnson home, and nothing came of it. But Johnson's wife and family decamped to Portland for a few days, just in case. The experience, understandably, rattled the Johnson household."[14]

In any other written account of this story, it would be astounding if the author did not comment on the danger to society posed by death threats against a city official and his family. Yet this point eludes Gibson. The logic of his book is such that the people who issue violent threats against the Johnson family are not only victims themselves, but victims more worthy of our concern than the Johnsons. While Gibson does not come right out and tell the reader to sympathize with the people who make death threats against Jim Johnson and his wife, he paints a portrait of a Christmas war conspirator who inflamed public passions by trampling on the sacred, then jets off to a professional conference to work on his career. The result is an understated portrait of a man who officiously drives people to lash out at him—an image of a new enemy who brings violent threats on himself.

The issue pushed off the stage by violent language in the "war on Christmas" debate is "culture." This debate is about teaching our children to respect the range of cultural practices in the world we inhabit, instead of remaking American society around the rituals of one religion.

At the heart of Gibson's "war" story lies a basic claim that distorts and taints discussions of religion and the public sphere, a claim that remains unstated until Gibson presents it boldly in his last chapter. Quoting a letter to the editor sent to a paper in Oregon from a reader named Anne Cutting, Gibson explains what it really means when Cutting calls for religion to be a more "private matter":

> That attitude demonstrates a desire on her part, and evidently on the part of others who feel like she does, to push Christianity into a place where it does not confront people, where it is hidden. Liberal crusaders are treating Christianity as if it were second hand smoke from cigarettes: segregate it, hide it, and wherever you can...ban it. To this point, there's a popular bumper sticker spotted around Eugene, Oregon, these days that reads, "So Many Christians, So Few Lions."[15]

The war Gibson claims exists is not just about Christmas decorations, but about the nature of American society itself. If the anti-Christmas factions win the war, then America will be transformed in an apartheid society. Through his book, readers are led to believe that Christianity will be coerced by law and by opprobrium to hide in the shadows and that Christian ritual will be beaten back into private spaces by marauding "crusaders." *The War on Christmas* is, in other words, a revised version of the reverse discrimination argument. It is based on the cynical lie that a supposedly disempowered majority is suffering from oppression or worse at the hands of an all powerful minority. Moreover, the anti-Christian threat to this country undermines the Constitution itself by suppressing freedom of speech, freedom of religion, and freedom of representation. It is a horrifying prospect, and Gibson delivers it with a glint in his eye. If only it were true.

What, then, is the more productive, pragmatic argument? Most Americans do not relish the prospect of the next fifty Decembers turning into non-stop, on-air gripe sessions by the likes of Gibson about how Christians are victims of anti-Christian forces waging war against them. To move beyond this distraction, however, requires an initial opening observation about the "war on Christmas" campaign that may seem counterintuitive at first:

the "war on Christmas" concerns neither "war" nor "Christmas," but culture.

In his attempt to define the tricky and oft-used term, historian of language Raymond Williams once described "culture" as "one of two or three of the most complicated words in the English language." "Culture" suggests a wide range of activities and ideas ranging from opera to novels and philosophy on the one hand, to traditional styles of dress or food on the other. Barbecue ribs are American "culture," as are Walt Whitman's poems and NASCAR. In other words, culture is a big idea. While it may be difficult to pin down an exact definition, one thing about culture is very clear: in the past few decades there has been a sea change in the way Americans understand it. Specifically, our country has shifted from the idea that there is one, monolithic set of habits, tastes, and ideas that we all share and which alone can be called "American culture," to a more flexible idea that American culture includes many different components, all of which somehow manage to fit together. Where once we looked at the world and saw different nations as distinct puzzle pieces, we now live in a world marked by an increasing overlap of cultures, languages, traditions, and religions. With each generation, the ability to compete and even function in a culturally interconnected world depends on a view of culture that goes beyond mere tolerance for cultural differences to actual acceptance that widespread difference is a normal state of affairs.

Still, despite this movement towards a more diverse and inclusive understanding of American culture, there are many recurrent moments and situations that cause us to think about the meaning of this diversity. In school, for example, teachers once accepted the canons and taught them year after year. Now teachers wrestle with the best way to assemble curriculums so that students learn key lessons from the history of American ideas. Class curriculums, as a result, have become focus points of engagement between parents and teachers about the best way to prepare children for the future—a healthy development. Similarly, workplaces at holiday times—once assumed to be simply containers for the display of a single idea of culture—have become points of discussion, often heated, about the best way to represent a given moment in the calendar. Although not without hiccups, this dialogue has also been a healthy development as it has engaged more and more people in discussions about the role of culture in the public square.

What can and should count as culture in the public square is, ultimately, the issue that Americans wrestle with at these times. It is a difficult question because there are some moments in the year when certain aspects of American culture appear to be so uniformly practiced that they give the impression to many of a multicultural America being temporarily turned on its head. In the end, though, the question we face about culture in the public square emerges from a very important distinction between government and non-government spaces and between culture and ritual. According to our Constitution, government may not endorse any single religion. This has not meant that all aspects of religious culture must be removed from every corner of every government building, but simply that we must be cautious about official government actions that appear to take the shape of religious ritual. A non-denominational benediction on the floor of Senate to start out a legislative session is different than, say, inviting a rabbi to perform a full morning service from the floor of the House of Representatives. In our system, sacred ritual plays no role in official governmental policy. And even though the challenge of finding the line between ritual and culture can be difficult at times, it is not impossible.

What remains, then, is the difference between culture and ritual in the public square—those arenas in our lives that are governed by constitutional principles and laws, but which are not typically guided by official government actions. How should the many facets of American culture take shape in the lobbies of our office buildings, in the passageways of our airports, in the waiting rooms of our hospitals and in our school lunchrooms? While the sheer range and scale of local communities in our democracy make any single outcome impossible, we can indicate two extremes that define the range of possibilities from (1) only one culture represented to (2) absolutely no culture represented whatsoever. Both of these extremes seem untenable. The best solution seems to lie somewhere in the middle.

In the instance where employees decide to decorate their offices, the default solution until recently was simply to festoon the lobby with Christmas decorations. Today, however, the challenge is neither to eliminate all decorations nor to reduce the variety of seasonal images down to Christian religious symbolism, but to find a way to broaden the ornamentation so that the many different symbols of the season celebrated by employees can be included. Having these debate is an important part of the civic process, and problems arise when we are pushed to exclude all but one culture, or to get rid of it all. Framing these discussions about culture in the public square in terms of "war" and "conspiracy" forces us down that frustrating road and away from what is truly important to us during the holiday season. More and more Americans seek to enrich civic spaces with a full range of cultural symbols, thereby folding all of our collective religious celebrations into the fabric of national life. The only challenge we face along this path is recognizing the difference between learning about the religion of others and officially endorsing one religion as government practice.

Nobody doubts the complexity of this challenge. For over two centuries, Protestantism has stood mostly alone as a source of cultural fixtures in the public square. Through a broad consensus over the past twenty years, however, Protestantism has made room for other religious traditions to contribute symbols, songs and celebrations to our national vocabulary. At the same time, the shift has revealed an assumption about American tradition as exclusively Protestant. This has never been the case. The reason for this new interest in diversity is not some fictive battle between religions or between believers and apostates, but a growing importance that Americans now give to preparing our children for the world as it is—a world where a sustainable future depends on dexterity with situations of immense cultural variation.

Teaching America's children the skills to excel in a world of confounding cultural diversity begins in schools. Not surprisingly, American school children often enjoy lessons about cultural diversity more than the classical subjects. Since children have vibrant imaginations and a healthy drive to discover the world, studying the exotic-sounding rituals and religious beliefs of new cultures is often more interesting to young students than studying prime numbers, indirect objects, and the boiling point of saltwater. Just the same, students can distinguish between cultural information as the content of a school lesson and religious ritual as official practice. Parents can make the same distinction and often do.

I remember for example, learning about Native American ritual during a cultural lesson at summer camp. As part of a group of nine and ten-year old Jewish kids from the suburbs of Detroit, Philadelphia and New York, we spent a month learning about local tribes in Maine, in the process making traditional native dress, and even performing a version of a local native dance, in between sailing, baseball and archery. At the end of the summer, my parents never worried that my camp counselors had forced me to abandon being Jewish and embrace Penobscot rituals and beliefs. And I did not worry either. Thirty years later, I can still tie a bowline knot, field a ground ball, and hit the front of a target from twenty yards out. And I have also never forgotten how important Native American culture is in Maine, and in every other state in the Union.

The debate about culture, in other words, is not a war, but an endless string of family conversations about the best way to educate children. With each passing year, more and more children in this country are facing a new kind of challenge in schools, summer camps and everywhere else their parents send them: the challenge of relating what they know about the world in which they were raised to a wide range of cultural information gleaned from books, exercises and activities. It is a challenge that inspires questions and imaginations, and which leaves memories that will stick along with a wide range of others. To conclude that such a challenge is too great for American children is not only a false argument, but expresses a profound pessimism in future generations.

7. CHILD OF PAIN

On August 23, 2004, James Dobson appeared on *Hannity and Colmes* to discuss his controversial book about training young children, *The New Strong-Willed Child*. Pro forma for his interviews on FOX, Dobson started off with a compliment to his hosts. Colmes then cut immediately to the question of violence as a "tool" in childcare, which was Dobson's defining issue as a professional giver of advice on parenting:

> COLMES: So under what conditions would you then use corporal punishment?
> DOBSON: In those circumstances, usually between about 2 and 10, where a child knows what you want, and not because he's made a mistake or he spilled his milk, or he's, you know, lost something. That's childish irresponsibility. But when that child looks you in the eye and says, "I know what you want and I'm not going to give it to you. I don't think you're tough enough to make me."
> COLMES: But are you then teaching a child, this is the way you deal with conflict resolution, with the hand, with the paddle? This is how you resolve—is that a lesson you want to teach kids?

> DOBSON: Absolutely. That's yielding to authority. You know, all of life is like this. I mean, a child crawls out over the edge of a high chair. He learns all about gravity in one lesson. He pulls a dog's tail, and he gets a little row of teeth marks. He touches a hot stove, and he gets burned. A child learns from that little bit of pain. Now, you don't want to take it to the extremes. You must not abuse a child.[1]

Many Americans are unaware of Dobson's long history as an author of advice books on the discipline of children. Since he first began writing in the early 1970s, his Christian-centered books on parenting have boasted millions of readers. Despite his central place as a parenting expert, Dobson is far better known as head of Focus on the Family, and for his daily radio show of the same name which reaches hundreds of millions of listeners worldwide and has served to define his public image in the past decade as a leading advocate of radical conservative social policy.

Even if it is not apparent at first glance, Dobson's views on seemingly divergent political issues find a common ground in the language and logic through which he locates and defends the place of violence in the American family. In this respect, Dobson's use of violence in his writing and speaking is one of the most subtle and far-reaching in contemporary America. He exemplifies the difference between political language that calls for violence and political language that defines issues in terms of violence. Distinguishing between these two categories of political speech—violent prescriptions and violent logic—is the key to reading and understanding the deep and troubling impact that Dobson has had on American political debate over the past decade. For example, during an appearance on *Hannity & Colmes* in 2003, one year prior to the previous example, Dobson commented on the importance for children of hitting back when picked on at school. His exchange with Sean Hannity reveals a remarkable ability to redefine issues through a logic of violence:

HANNITY: ... And I said, well, I tell my son that if anyone hits him it would be OK to hit back. And my—actually, the teacher at my son's school heard it and called my wife at home, was very upset that I said that. Is that what you mean in what we were discussing with Pat?

DOBSON: Well, it is part of what I mean and I agree completely with you, Sean. Kids can be brutal to each other. If you haven't hung around kids very long, you may not know that. But they can be...

HANNITY: They can be mean to each other.

DOBSON: ... they can brutalize each other. And bully each other. And to leave a kid absolutely helpless, to stand there while that's going on is a mistake. You can teach him to turn the other cheek later. But not when he's in elementary school.

HANNITY: If somebody puts their hand on a child then it's appropriate. And I told—my wife agrees with me. She thinks—but she goes, you've got to make certain that he understands only if force is brought to him.

DOBSON: Right. Right, you shouldn't be the aggressor. You must not be the aggressor but if somebody is hitting you...

HANNITY: You've got the right to punch him back.

DOBSON: You've got to defend yourself.

HANNITY: But in this day and age you'll be thrown out of every school in the country.

DOBSON: Well, that may be but there are some things that are right.[2]

In this exchange, Hannity offers a basic pitch for the value of teaching one's children to hit back at school—a point that he claims is highly controversial. Dobson then uses this starting point to introduce a hitherto unheard of distinction in Christ's famous "turn the other cheek" lesson. Since childhood is brutal, according to Dobson, the key for children is to learn first to fight back, and only then, after they are old enough to understand that fighting back against aggression is the right thing to do, should they learn to turn the other cheek. Dobson then goes even further to suggest that American public schools themselves violate this basic rule of early childhood development by hindering the ability of young boys to respond to schoolyard violence with more violence. In the process, he blames "feminists and others" for trying to make boys more like girls. In Dobson's hands, concepts as fundamental to politics as school and education become redefined through a logic of violence—in this case gender, Christianity and violence. While Dobson never says that boys should be taught to fight in schools, he does say that children are "brutal" to each other and that all children should defend themselves from "aggression," thereby implying that all children must learn to defend themselves from the violence that awaits them at the hands of their peers in school.

Dobson's many appearances on *Hannity & Colmes* spoke to a convergence of factors in American politics and media that made him a star in both realms. Although historians at some future date will clarify the true impact of the Religious Right on the 2000 and 2004 presidential election outcomes, conventional wisdom declared it the X factor that delivered and kept George W. Bush in power. As always, the conventional wisdom masks a more complicated story. Dobson's rise was not just about religious voters, but the sign of a changing of the public voice of Christians who made up a particularly strident base of the Republican Party. In the 1980s, the Christian leaders who dominated Republican Party politics called themselves a "moral majority" and brought an old version of evangelical Baptism to bear on the media. The power of men like Jerry Falwell and Pat Robertson was their ability to turn the TV into the greatest collection plate in history, thereby amassing enough financial and political capital to build new institutions, including mega-churches and universities. And yet, as important as the rise of the Moral Majority was in delivering victory to Ronald Reagan in

1980, the leadership never fully achieved the strong cultural position that their political achievements would suggest. With their southern drawls, tin smiles, and constant pitch for donations, the public distrusted the early leaders of the Religious Right even as their political influence and achievements grew. Falwell and Robertson were both seen as preachers from Virginia who had made it big on TV. As such, neither ever fully shook off the image of the pastor who came to town preaching miracles and turned millionaire in the process.

Dobson was different. He was an evangelical, not a Southern Baptist. Born, raised and educated in California, he built a foothold for his movement in the American West. More importantly, Dobson was not a preacher, but a licensed clinical professional. Before his rise to national political and media prominence during the Bush administration, the biggest feather in Dobson's cap had been serving as one of nine experts on the controversial Attorney General's Commission on Pornography assembled by President Reagan. Dobson's biography in the 1986 final report is as impressive for it's listing of professional accomplishment as for the expert way it frames Dobson's career in strictly neutral, non-religious terms:

> Dr. James Dobson received a Bachelor of Arts degree in psychology from Pasadena College in 1958. He was awarded a Master of Science degree from the University of Southern California in 1962. He earned a Ph.D. from U.S.C. in 1967 in Child Development and Research Design. Dr. Dobson served for fourteen years as Associate Clinical Professor of Pediatrics at the University of Southern California School of Medicine, and simultaneously, for seventeen years on the Attending Staff of Children's Hospital of Los Angeles, in the Division of Medical Genetics. He was also Director of Behavioral Research in the Division of Child Development during a portion of this time. More recently, Dr. Dobson has been President of Focus on the Family, a non-profit organization dedicated to the preservation of the home.[3]

The biography goes on to mention recognition by President Carter and previous appointments by President Reagan. Were it not for the vague labeling of Focus on the Family as a "non-profit organization dedicated to the preservation of the home," the biography could be the description of any of a dozen senior-level university academics with crossover careers in public service. Lurking behind the phrasing, however, was Dobson's obsession with turning his version of a Christian-inspired, patriarchal family into the DNA of a new authoritarian America—an America where parents use pain aversion to train their children to respect the moral order of the family hierarchy. To "preserve the home" means, for Dobson, to rebuild America one family at a time, transforming society and culture in the process.

Much of Dobson's focus in the past few years has been on the violence that he believes homosexuality commits against the institution of marriage. In his most recent book, *Marriage Under Fire: Why We Must Win This Battle*, Dobson frames marriage in violent terms and takes the metaphor of political debate as warfare to an alarmist level. Elaborating on a purported forty-year "master plan" by homosexual activists to "utterly destroy the family," Dobson compares the push for equal marriage rights in America to Hitler's military conquest of Europe:

> Like Adolf Hitler, who overran his European neighbors, those who favor homosexual marriage are determined to make it legal, regardless of the democratic processes that stand in the way.[4]

Rather than saying explicitly that equal rights activists are violent, Dobson relies on his reader to remember that Hitler rose to power by burning down the Reichstag, building concentration camps, and carrying out the industrial genocide of European Jewry. Thus, *Marriage Under Fire* gives voice to Dobson's signature style of social and cultural arguments. First he names the policies he opposes, then claims those policies will lead to the downfall of civilization:

> Admittedly, there have been periods in history when homosexuality has flourished, as in the biblical cities of Sodom and Gomorrah, in Ancient Greece and in the Roman Empire. None of these civilizations survived.[5]

Of course, civilizations do not die because of one social factor, be it sexual practices or any other single variable. Dobson's argument in *Marriage Under Fire* is such a simplistic, political just-so story that it would earn him a failing grade in most middle school history classes. As a means of political debate, however, the book's strength is Dobson's relentless use of violent metaphors through which the words "marriage" and "homosexuality" become historic foes engaged in an epic battle for survival. The theme is carried through even at the visual level of book design, as a stylized image of rifle cross-hairs recur throughout the book to remind the reader that the "homosexual agenda" will not just destroy marriage, it will also shoot to kill. As a result, saving America from total destruction of fascist and biblical proportions will require a political commitment equal to an armed defense of the nation.

It is his ultimate, far-reaching utopian goal to save America—marriage by marriage, child by child, home by home—that renders even the most seemingly trivial matters in Dobson's work highly political. When writing about homosexuality, he describes how it will destroy everything of concern to the contemporary reader, thus resulting in collapse of healthcare, Social Security, education, religion and, most notably, the widespread suffering of children. This logic is not new. Dobson's first and most famous book, *Dare To Discipline*, first published in 1970 and reissued multiple times, is not only a key to his thinking in his later books and polemics, but a Rosetta Stone for most of his authoritarian logic. *Dare to Discipline* is about the careful use of violence and pain by parents to train their children in the context of a loving family. However, when read in the context of the past eight years, *Dare To Discipline* can be seen as a foreshadowing of much of the rhetoric used by the Bush-Cheney administration to sell the "War on Terror."

Of all the examples of right-wing pundits who write and speak about politics in a violent idiom, *Dare To Discipline* is perhaps the most startling because it uses violence to describe the non-violent behavior of preschool children. For Dobson, a child who misbehaves is not just naughty, but a "tyrant and dictator" whose behavior threatens not only the peace and quiet of his parents, but the viability of the family and the nation.[6] In other words, the solution to the "potent weapon" of a child's defiance is loving discipline, by which Dobson means the "deliberate, premeditated application of minor pain to a small child."[7] Simply beating a child is wrong and a point Dobson makes repeatedly in *Dare to Discipline*. The goal of loving discipline is not just to show that the parent is superior to the child, but to "win decisively" when a toddler knowingly defies a parent's authority. To illustrate this distinction, Dobson recounts an instance from his own childhood where his mother thrashed him with her girdle:

> The day I learned the importance of staying out of reach shines like a neon light in my mind. I made the costly mistake of sassing her when I was about four feet away. I knew I had crossed the line and wondered what she would do about it. It didn't take long to find out. Mom wheeled around to grab something with which to express her displeasure, and her hand landed on a girdle. Those were the days when a girdle was lined with rivets and mysterious panels. She drew back and swung the abominable garment in my direction, and I can still hear it whistling through the air. The intended blow caught me across the chest, followed by a multitude of straps and buckles, wrapping themselves around my midsection. She gave me an entire thrashing

with one blow! But from that day forward, I measured my words carefully when addressing my mother. I never spoke disrespectfully to her again, even when she was seventy-five years old.[8]

It is an astounding story, and Dobson uses it to define a core concept in childrearing that subsequently translates into his politics: children can be trained to respect authority through the sudden and swift application of sharp pain. Disciplining a child with pain in these moments is not just about dealing with a specific moment of sassiness, but is the first step in "disarming the teenage time-bomb…twelve years before it arrives."[9] For Dobson, discipline is a pre-emptive strike against the enemy, or as he put it, "If discipline begins on the second day of life, you're one day late."[10]

Given that Dobson believes life begins at conception, the conclusion is that the discipline of children by pain is not merely a way to remedy bad behavior, but an opportunity to express love. According to Dobson, the best chance to communicate comes after an episode where the parent has physically hurt the child:

For this reason, parents should not dread or shrink back from confrontations with their children. These occasions should be anticipated as important events, because they provide the opportunity to convey verbal and nonverbal messages to the boy or girl that cannot be expressed at other times.[11]

To bring a toddler to tears by hitting them on the legs with a wooden switch or squeezing their trapezius muscle gives parents an "opportunity" to express their love. While the child recovers from the pain, parents then tell them about "the importance of obedience."[12] In stark contrast to other parenting methods, Dobson argues that parents must first "win decisively" a "nose-to-nose" confrontation with a child. Only after such victories should a parent talk about the virtues of obedience, but never before. The results are a child who learns that a failure to obey authority results in immediate, temporary pain, and a quiet and orderly household. In other words, the violence that a parent lovingly anticipates and dishes out on a toddler is the proper response to the child's "weapon" of choice: insolence. Failure to win decisively in these moments has disastrous consequences when the child reaches adolescence and adulthood.

Dobson's discussion of pain as a parenting technique gives rise to a catalogue of contemporary social problems that emerge when a parent fails to train a toddler to yield to their authority. In particular, when faced with criticism that the pain techniques advocated in *Dare To Discipline* will actually teach children to use violence to dominate others, Dobson responds that a parent's failure to use loving violent discipline on a child will actually lead the child to become violent toward the parent. In a description of a child he names "Becky," the parents' failure to use physical pain to enforce their authority results in an adolescent public enemy whose violent outbursts turn directly on the permissive mother. Violent tantrums, thus, give rise to a household ruled by fear of the child's anger and potential to engage in domestic battering. In an effort to correct their mistakes, the parents who failed to discipline Becky with pain when she was a toddler try in vain to satisfy her adolescent rebelliousness with gifts and parties:

> They thought a party might make her happy, and Mrs. Holloway worked very hard to decorate the house and prepare refreshments. On the appointed evening, a mob of dirty, profane teens swarmed into the house, breaking and destroying the furnishings. During the course of the evening, Mrs. Holloway said something that angered Becky. The girl struck her mother and left her lying in a pool of blood in the bathroom.[13]

Discipline by pain, or lack thereof in the case of Becky and the Holloways, becomes a nexus between parenting and politics. Dobson tells parents to either pre-empt the adolescent violence of their children by hurting the toddler, or to suffer the consequences of their "parental failures" later on as they lie face down in a pool of their own blood. If this discipline by pain does not happen, the violence of the adolescent will eventually rise up to rule the parents' lives. Moreover, warns Dobson, the rein of fear caused by the undisciplined child will spread damage to property and to civil society. When violent discipline of the child is successful, however, the parent trains the child to forever yield to authority, thereby controlling their destructive urges. The household that emerges from this dynamic that Dobson sets up is not ruled by the fear of adolescent children, but balanced by a counterweight fear of pain from the parents. Society benefits from such homes, according to Dobson, because the proper balance of childhood obedience and parental authority imbues the home with the "God-fearing" quality necessary for the family to serve as the divine building block of society, as well as the nation, as Christ intended. A parent's use of pain to train a child thereby demonstrates a boundary between the sacred and the profane.

Discipline is the dividend of violence used correctly, sparingly and lovingly. To the extent that Americans have a position on the responsible use of pain as an incentive in parenting, most would see no problem with a quick spank on a child's bottom to scurry them out of playing in busy street or a slap on a child's hand to stop them from grabbing a hot stove. Spanking as a quick tactic for protecting children from danger, however, is a far cry from a broad cultural, social and governmental program that begins with the use of pain to train children to obey parental authority. The distinction is not difficult to grasp, but it is one that Dobson often tries to blur, claiming that liberals oppose his approach to discipline because they are against all instances of spanking and against teaching children any form of respect for authority. Despite the fact that Dobson, too, believes that a quick slap on the bottom can be a useful tool for spontaneously protecting kids from danger, his view of spanking is strategic, which he describes in specific terms in *Dare to Discipline*:

> My point is that the principles in this book are not designed to produce perfect little robots who can sit with their hands folded in the parlor thinking patriotic and noble thoughts! Even if we could pull that off, it wouldn't be wise to try. The objective, as I see it, is to take the raw material with which our babies arrive on this earth, and then gradually mold it into mature, responsible, and God-fearing adults. It is a twenty-year process that will bring progress, setbacks, success, and failures.[14]

Spanking, thus, is not intended merely to eliminate behavior in children that may bother an adult, but instead creates parent-child relationships that mimic Dobson's conception of the relationship between people and God. That is, spanking produces adults who are "God-fearing." The threat and use of pain by a parent on their child brings fear into the home and gives it a central place in the formation of the child's personality. When that fear vanishes from the home, according to Dobson, it is a parenting failure that results in a breakdown of both a child's personality and society as a whole. This breakdown leads to delinquency, crime, abortion and worst of all, gender identity disorder.

The connection between the painful disciplining of toddlers and Dobson's views on homosexuality are often overlooked. According to Dobson, homosexuality is not an inherited trait, but a disorder that begins with a condition called "prehomosexuality."[15] This condition first begins to manifest itself at about thirty months of age, which is the exact time in a young boy's life that Dobson claims painful discipline is necessary. During this period, if the parents fail to notice a child's prehomosexuality, or allow it to go untreated, the condition can develop into full-blown "gender identity disorder"—a term borrowed from clinical psychologist Joseph Nicolosi and a

Dobsonism for gay. The most important sign of prehomosexuality is pronounced and repeated "feminine behavior" in male toddlers. Dobson references this quote from Nicolosi:

> The fact is, there is a high correlation between feminine behavior in boyhood and adult homosexuality. There are telltale signs of discomfort with . . . Boys and deep-seated and disturbing feelings that they [are] different and somehow inferior. And yet parents often miss the warning signs and wait too long to seek help for their children. One reason for this is that they are not being told the truth about their children's gender confusion, and they have no idea what to do about it.[17]

Homosexuality, in other words, has origins not just in the behavior of a child, but the failure of the parents to manage the child correctly. It is a disorder that results, Dobson claims, not so much from sex, but from a parenting failure exacerbated by the so-called political agenda of gays and lesbians. Ultimately, while Dobson thinks homosexuality is wrong based on scriptural grounds, that claim alone masks both the violence and politics of his viewpoint. It is the use of pain in child rearing that leads to the creation of God-fearing families, which in turn leads to happy and productive American citizens. To give in to the supposed liberal ideology of permissiveness results in failure as a parent, departure from God's ways, unhappiness and ultimately a painful life for the individual. Bringing pain into the parenting process keeps pain away later in life.

If the parenting is successful, parents will be in a position to recognize "prehomosexuality" should it emerge in their child, and then see to it that the child makes the proper "choice" about their sexuality. For boys in particular, this process leads Dobson to suggest some fathering techniques that at first glance seem out of place with the common stereotype of evangelical sexual mores:

Meanwhile, the boy's father has to do his part. He needs to mirror and affirm his son's maleness. He can play rough-and-tumble games with his son, in ways that are decidedly different from the games he would play with a little girl. He can help his son learn to throw and catch a ball. He can teach him to pound a square wooden peg into a square hole in a pegboard. He can even take his son with him into the shower, where the boy cannot help but notice that Dad has a penis, just like his, only bigger.[18]

The scene of a two-year old boy looking at his father's penis in the shower may seem at first glance to have nothing to do with corporal punishment. Moreover, it raises a fascinating question that reveals how central Dobson's authoritarian parenting techniques are to every other aspect of his politics. In other words, put a naked father and his naked son in a shower—the younger looking at the penis of the elder—and that situation may not be homosexual, per se, but it is certainly a homosocial moment about gender and sex. So what leads this moment to produce a heterosexual boy with the right impulses, according to Dobson, as opposed to a homosexual male with the wrong desires?

The answer to that question is parents who dared to discipline their children. For this "notice-that-dad-has-a-penis" shower moment to be effective, Dobson explains that it must be performed by a father who has previously used painful discipline on his son to establish authority. Such a father has presumably begun to build up in his son the beginnings of God-fearing adulthood. In the absence of responsibly violent disciplinary parenting, the father-son shower scene would just become another form of liberal lewdness. Parenting that does not include corporal discipline results in the "choice" a young boy makes to transform his pre-homosexuality into gender identity disorder.

The issue nudged off the table by the violent language in the parenting debate is "community." The debate is about the optimism of healthy communities, versus the pessimism of extreme individualism.

Dobson's political rhetoric—whether he is talking about homosexuality, tax policy or foreign wars—ultimately returns to the idea that a strong and moral America depends entirely on families where heterosexual parents use pain to establish authority over their children. The obedient child—specifically the obedient son, as Dobson is much less concerned about women—becomes the essential building block of a God-fearing America. Critics who focus too much attention on Dobson's descriptions of how to use pain in parenting fail to understand his corrosive influence on American political debate. His rhetoric follows a strong internal logic that leads people to a false conclusion about American society in general via a specific common experience with unruly children. Even those Americans who do not yet have children can understand the claim that children who do not respect authority in the home will grow up to not respect authority out of the home. And like all good political arguments, whether or not Dobson's argument is actually true is not necessarily as important as whether or not it is persuasive.

As a result, Dobson's view of the disciplined, God-fearing child who has made the correct gender choices undermines political discussions in ways that are far more pervasive than the initial discussion of spanking toddlers implies. Nowhere is this more explicit than in his political pronouncements on foreign policy. When considered in light of Dobson's writings on parenting and homosexuality, his descriptions of the national security problems America faces take on an entirely new level of meaning. For example, several months prior to the 2006 midterm elections, Dobson delivered a speech at the Values Voter Summit.[19] His core argument in the speech was that fighting the "War on Terror" was equivalent to fighting against a "family crisis" in America. The speech was infused with descriptions of failed policy that echoed Dobson's critiques of failed, overly permissive parenting:

> Would you favor turning the leadership of this nation over to those who believe we can negotiate with extremists and talk them into being "nice"? And can we avoid a showdown simply by packing up and running away? Diplomacy has its place, of course, but trying to negotiate with those who want to kill us is ridiculous.[20]

Thus foreign policy, like raising children, is about using discipline to establish authority. Just like dealing with a defiant child who acts like a "tyrant" or "dictator," dealing with an actual tyrant or dictator on the world stage demands a nose-to-nose confrontation, not a head-to-head talk. This kind of foreign policy ideology would have powerful resonance with anyone who has raised their children according to Dobson's principles. In addition to mirroring his own parenting logic, Dobson also brings the consequences of failed parenting and his anti-homosexual agenda to foreign policy, particularly in his description of U.S. elected officials who failed to speak up in the wake of Hugo Chavez' public critiques of President Bush:

> What should infuriate every American is that hardly any congressmen or senators stepped forward to condemn this outrage with the passion it warranted. What kind of wimps have we become when the elected leader of this great nation can be assaulted in our own country and no one has the guts to condemn it vehemently? I heard a former ambassador talking on Fox News after the Chavez statement. His limp-wristed response was that America should work harder to make friends around the world. It made me sick.[21]

According to Dobson, the entire Congress seems to have come down with a bad case of prehomosexuality. And, as we know from

CHILD OF PAIN

his writings, homosexuality flourishes in society as a result of failed authoritarian parenting.

What would be a good starting point for getting past the rhetoric and logic Dobson relentlessly pumps into the debate? First, it is important to consider the gaping flaw in his theory—and it is a theory, not a fact—which is that the authoritarian family is the building block of a strong America. There is no question that the authoritarian family is a building block for authoritarian organizations like Focus on the Family, or even for an authoritarian America. But a strong America? In general, social theories that pin all their hopes to one variable are not true. Dobson's is not true either. The problem in his theory is that strong societies depend on a wide array of factors working together, not a single dynamic, be it parental, disciplinary, or otherwise. Families are important to American society, but Dobson would have us see the family unit in isolation. Yet, progressives, liberals and conservatives alike generally view the building blocks of a strong society as much larger than the single household. The more common view is that a strong America is built from thriving communities, which have many components working together. Each family contributes in its own way to a community and the ways in which those communities may flourish vary. Thus, there are many kinds of thriving communities that make up a strong America.

No matter what the community, however, the key has always been for individuals and individual families to stand together and look out for the well-being of one other. As Alexis de Tocqueville famously wrote in the 1830s, the great secret of American progress is the ability of its citizens to form associations that work together towards common goals that are greater than the sum of their parts:

> Americans of all ages, all stations in life, and all types of disposition are forever forming associations. There are not only commercial and industrial associations in which all take part, but others of a thousand different types—reli-

145

gious, moral, serious, futile, very general and very limited, immensely large and very minute. . . In democratic countries knowledge of how to combine is the mother of all other forms of knowledge; on its progress depends that of all the others.[22]

After "associations," the most important word in the quote from Tocqueville is "progress." In Dobson's lament about the harmful impact parents effect when they fail to discipline their children, one hardly notices that he fails to talk about progress, a core principle of American society. This is because Dobson's vision for society does not focus on progress, but on obedience, which his why he so often repeats the term "God-fearing" as an ideal. Belief in God and progress should not be at odds with one other, but it is difficult to see them as compliments in Dobson's fear and punishment rhetoric.

Forming associations with an eye towards a common goal is an original feature of American society that began on the boat ride from England. The Mayflower Compact , written at sea and signed upon landing, mentions "God" and "Christian faith" many times. However, the purpose of the Mayflower Compact was not to establish a religious organization but a "civil Body Politick" to guarantee "better ordering and preservation and furtherance." As Hannah Arendt describes in her masterful analysis of the history of American political philosophy *On Revolution*, the centrality of the Mayflower Compact in American culture emerged not just from its ability to bring people together, but from its role in establishing a tradition of voluntary covenants aimed at overcoming fear:

The really astounding fact in the whole story is that their obvious fear of one another was accompanied by the no less obvious confidence they had in their own power, granted and confirmed by no one and as yet unsupported by any means of violence, to combine themselves together into a "civil Body Politick" which, held together solely by the strength of mutual promise "in the Presence of God and one another," supposedly was powerful enough to "enact, constitute, and frame" all necessary laws and instruments of government. This deed quickly became a precedent.[23]

It is that strength of mutual promise—without violence—on which thriving and lasting communities emerge and on which America depends. As Arendt points out so eloquently, the decision to enter into mutual compacts was the political ground on which the framing of constitutions took place. The decision of these strangers on a boat was to look at each other and see that their ability to overcome fear and survive nature would depend on their forming a body larger than themselves, greater than the family or the home—a body politic.

The next question was how to establish enduring forms and rules for running that body. The answer was a period of constitutional framing that served as the imperfect but as yet unrivaled launch of the American states and subsequent national union. Thus, in the time even before the beginning of the United States, it was not discipline or Christianity or narrow focus on the family that kept the Pilgrims strong: it was faith in each other.

Recently, the American tradition of faith in each other has been taken up by a progressive interest in the "common good," a fundamentally American principle that has been buried beneath decades of aggressive right-wing talk about the necessity of separating individual citizens from government. In Dobson's discussion about corporal punishment, it is difficult to see that a overly insular focus on the family can be detrimental to raising children who are happy, productive, disciplined, and who go on to lead lives full of meaning. It is easier, perhaps, to start at a distance from the family and with a topic that involves the common good in a more obvious way.

During his presidency, Lyndon Johnson, spoke frequently about the environment as a shared "national heritage." In a speech he gave on the occasion of signing the "Water Quality Act of 1965," for example, Johnson exemplified this view of America rooted in the notion of community, rather than isolated individualism:

> The clear, fresh waters that were our national heritage have become dumping grounds for garbage and filth. They poison our fish; they breed disease; they despoil our landscapes. No one has a right to use America's rivers and America's waterways that belong to all the people as a sewer. The banks of a river may belong to one man or even one industry or one State, but the waters which flow between those banks should belong to all the people.[24]

In moments of national crisis, Americans seek balance between the individual and the commons, between families and community. Indeed, the Constitution of the United States was itself written with this complex sense of balance in mind. The foundation of our system of government is coequal branches, as well as a balance between individual states and the collective union of the republic. We passionately defend individual liberties, but we balance them with the well-being of families and communities. Former Vice President Al Gore, the most prominent voice in the movement to reduce carbon levels in the atmosphere, extended this theme of the common good to a global conception of shared responsibility and shared interests. Speaking about the urgency of individuals working in concert to reduce the causes of global warming, Gore wrote, "There is only one Earth, and all of us who live on it share a common future."[25] The discussion of the environment is a good place to start to see how the "common good" frame defines discussion because the logic of the environmental debate is familiar to most of us. Within this debate, individuals are encouraged to see their behavior as effecting more than just their own lives or even the lives of their families. To conserve the environment and clean up pollution in the atmosphere, the key is for individuals to see their actions as helping or harming the community. In the 1970s, the environmental debate focused on the individual act of throwing trash in a garbage can instead of throwing it on the ground. The purpose of that discussion was to focus individuals on the consequences that their actions had for the entire country. Every American kid who lived through the 1970s remembers the famous television commercial where Iron Eyes Cody, in Native American dress, rides his horse through a riverbed strewn with garbage, whereupon the camera shows a tear rolling down his cheek. The public service announcements for the "Keep America Beautiful" campaign reframed how millions of American children came to understand that their personal actions affected the community as a whole.

Thirty years later, we have gone through a similar learning experience with regard to separating our garbage out into various types. We learned that throwing all of our trash into one can was also harmful to the environment, and that it was an individual's responsibility to the common good to place recyclable garbage in the proper canister. In time, Americans will learn how to manage the disposal of carbon emissions in a similar manner. While that campaigns has yet to fully begin, the "common good" frame will again help us to see that how our individual behavior results in carbon emissions. With innovations in technology and public service narratives to help us understand the best way to act in the interest of the common good, we will learn to manage this newest aspect of pollution. As we can see, the "common good" frame informs the entire environmental discussion—past, present, and future.

What is so fascinating about framing the environmental debate, however, is that the "common good" frame extends far beyond the issue of managing pollution. Ultimately, environmentalism is as much a moral debate about American citizenship as it is a debate about throwing away trash. Through the conversation about the environment, we teach our children a basic Jeffersonian lesson about the privilege and responsibility of adulthood in American democracy. In Thomas Jefferson's view, this balance was the essence of a new political system whereby each person played a role not just as an individual in private life, but as "participators" in the public realm.[26] The goal of Jefferson's democratic system was not to quash the individual or subsume the family within some broader collective concept, but to orient each citizen towards the dual role of individuality and public happiness. The result of this vision has been a political system capable of accomplishing great tasks over time. This enduring success has always asked of its citizens that they look beyond the individual and the individual family to dedicate themselves to the community at large or, as what Jefferson called the "sacred" principle" of "the common good."[27]

We can now see more clearly how such a conception of the "common good" brings us to a radically different notion of what it means for children to behave than the corporal punishment views of James Dobson. Strict obedience to parents may be the tradition of a given family, but obedience to parents cannot be the full range of factors that make up a healthy transition from childhood to adulthood because it lacks dedication to the common good. In this respect, the vast, practical challenges of repairing and sustaining the nation depends on a balance between respect for oneself, one's family, one's community and the common good.

8. THE WAR AGAINST THE WAR

On February 9, 2007, author and policy pundit Dinesh D'Souza appeared on *Your World With Neil Cavuto* to discuss how the media was portraying the U.S. military presence in Iraq. After a brief opening discussion about a photo of an Iraqi woman he had seen in *The New York Times* and another photo of U.S. troops that he had seen in *USA Today*, Cavuto concluded that the media was "portraying our troops in Iraq" in a bad light. Asked for his opinion, D'Souza kicked it up a notch, transforming Cavuto's opening point about pictures in various newspapers into a discussion of the real threat Americans faced on the home front:

> I think that certain segments of the media, *The New York Times* being a perfect example, are waging what can be called a war against the war on terror. Now, if they don't like it, they can say so on the editorial page, but this war is being conducted on the news page. The way it's conducted is that bad news is magnified, and good news is suppressed. A few months ago, the U.S. military uncovered documents from al Qaeda in Iraq basically saying that al Qaeda was losing the war. They had—no longer had the ability to fundamentally

destabilize the government. This was reported in *The Times*, but buried.[1]

Cavuto had asked D'Souza to comment on pictures in the newspaper, but D'Souza responded instead by reframing the media debate as an internal "war" against the United States government, the "war against the war on terror." So what is worse? The war or the war against the war? D'Souza's deftly placed comment steered the conversation right into that confusion, leaving the viewer to conclude that the danger America faces from newspaper reporting is on par—and in cahoots with—the insurgency our soldiers face in Iraq. Even though it only lasted a few minutes, D'Souza's conversation with Cavuto turned into an accusation that the media was working alongside al Qaeda to defeat our soldiers in Iraq and humiliate us at home.

A few days later, D'Souza made his way over to *The O'Reilly Factor* and used the same tactic to turn a conversation with Bill O'Reilly into a description of how the American left has teamed up with Osama bin Laden to destroy America:

> D'Souza: Bin Laden used to attack America as the generic enemy. In the last few years he's been doing something very strange. He's praising specific leftists in America and offering them a kind of truce. Basically, what he is saying is I will supply the terror, and you use the terror to demoralize the American people so that they will pull out of not only Iraq but the entire Middle East.[2]

Not satisfied solely with D'Souza's accusation against the contemporary American left and their collusion with terrorists to destroy the United States, O'Reilly invited D'Souza to relate his point back to the history of the Vietnam War:

> O'REILLY: I don't understand why the radical left wants

to pull away from the war on terror. I never got that. I can understand the Iraq war. But the overall war on terror?

D'SOUZA: Here's why. Think about the Vietnam War. We say America lost the Vietnam War. But I would say that the left won the Vietnam War. Why? The left wanted America to retreat in humiliation, and we did.[3]

The right-wing hobbyhorse about the anti-war movement as the cause for losing the war in Vietnam is familiar, but D'Souza translates it into something new. America, he explains, did not lose the Vietnam War. Rather, the American left teamed up with the enemy to win the war. Apparently, the left's war against the war in Iraq is not the first time liberals have teamed up with violent enemies to humiliate and defeat America.

D'Souza's appearances on FOX News in early 2007 were part of a broader publicity campaign for his new book, *The Enemy At Home: The Cultural Left and It's Responsibility for 9/11*, about the fight against terrorism and the root causes for the attacks of September 11, 2001. Anyone who continues to question how far the right will go to reframe politics in violent logic and language need only glance through D'Souza's book to be quickly and unceremoniously stripped of any remaining doubt.

Hailed as a "top young public policy maker," D'Souza is the kind of intellectual that is rare on the left, but very common on the right. He began his career on the *Dartmouth Review* of the 1980s, after which he was hired as a policy adviser in the Reagan administration. He now spends his time at the Hoover Institute. Interestingly enough, D'Souza's early writings were quite entertaining, if only for the gleeful ease by which he tied liberal intellectuals in knots. His wildly successful book of essays, *Letters To a Young Conservative*, grabbed hold of the time-honored genre of epistolary social commentary and dragged it into the age of confrontational satirical journalism.[4] Despite being a book-length slap in the face to American liberalism, with particular disdain for university-based liberal intellectuals, *Letters to a Young Conservative* is full of first-hand insight into campus conservatives' worldview, social objects and tactics. D'Souza may have displayed skill as a right-wing political trickster in his earlier works, but after 9/11, he dove into the deep end of the violent right.

I was in a Barnes and Noble near Lincoln Center in New York City the first time I caught sight of *The Enemy at Home* and my initial reaction was to laugh out loud and keep on walking. "Funny," I muttered to myself. "I thought al Qaeda was responsible for 9/11." But then I turned back and snatched the book off the shelf, dragging it to a quiet corner of the store for inspection. By my estimate, the cover of D'Souza's book alone accused roughly half of America of being violent criminals responsible for mass murder. And if "the cultural left" was "responsible" for the crimes of 9/11, then the cultural left would be guilty of treason a thousand of times over, a crime punishable by death. The accusation is, of course, patently false.

What I found shocking was not just that someone would write a book describing liberals as the cause behind one of the most heinous crimes in history, but that this accusation had earned the tacit consent of large, commercial publishers and distributors, such that it ended up in a prominent bookstore, display with all the innocence of a book on Origami napkin folding or a DVD of *Little Women*.

At its core, *The Enemy at Home* reframes American politics in the language and logic of war—specifically a civil war—to lay blame on the left for 9/11:

> The two major parties have become strange to each other in a way that America has not seen since 1860, when one faction saw slavery as a "positive good" and the other saw it as an entrenched evil. Now, as then, the two sides have difficulty recognizing each other as legitimate, as fully American, as possessing the same moral decency that we all take for granted in ourselves.[5]

In the familiar vein that marked the most vicious debates about morality in the 1980s, D'Souza sees politics in America not in terms of two parties, but two lifestyles—one "urban" and one "rural"—in constant and irreconcilable battle with each other for control of the nation.[6] According to D'Souza, the divide emerged after World War II, when more and more Americans walked away from a "traditional code of external morality" and embraced a lifestyle of rampant debauchery.[7] D'Souza is not particularly original or interesting in this part of his argument, adding little to what the likes of Pat Robertson and James Dobson have said before: conservatives believe in "family values," liberals believe there are no values, essentially, moral good versus moral relativism. It is a tired, old, false dichotomy.

The opposition between conservative values and liberals without values changes, however, in Chapter 3, entitled "America Through Muslim Eyes." There, D'Souza performs a bizarre act of make-believe anthropology by reading transcripts of letters written by jihadist suicide bombers and by Osama bin Laden himself in order to reconstruct the so-called "Muslim" reasoning for al Qaeda's attacks on 9/11. The result is a bit like turning to the Unibomber's writings as the basis for critiquing consumer society. This obvious flaw in methodology does not stop D'Souza. He claims that al Qaeda is not fighting against the United States, but defending itself against the violent advances of liberal depravity on a global scale. The reason for the suicide airplane bombings of 9/11, in other words, was not the intrusion of American foreign policy in the Middle East, but the slow war of immoral American culture against Islam:

> Contrary to the assertions of many on the left and even some on the right, bin Laden's primary objection is not to American foreign policy. The suicide bombers of radical Islam are not blowing themselves up because they are distressed over the Gulf War of 1991 or because they are in solidarity with the Palestinians...America, he asserts is "the modern world's symbol of paganism."[8]

As evidence for his argument that bin Laden is obsessed with attacking the United States because liberals have overrun world culture with "paganism," D'Souza digs ups quotes from bin Laden's 2002 "Letter to America." In that text, D'Souza claims to find evidence that bin Laden is primarily engaged in a cultural war with liberal values, which he mistakes for American values. In particular, D'Souza quotes bin Laden as saying that he ordered the attacks on 9/11 because, "You are a nation that exploits women like consumer products," and "you separate religion from your policies."

Oddly, D'Souza pulls out what he claims is a logical culture war narrative from bin Laden's letter. It is odd because bin Laden's actual letter is filled with the outlandish claims of a mass murdering megalomaniac. D'Souza correctly notes that bin Laden wrote about his offense at the "immorality and debauchery" that he sees in American culture. Yet, D'Souza left out the next lines in bin Laden's letter, which put those claims in context: "It is saddening to tell you that you are the worst civilization witnessed by the history of mankind."[9] Does that seem like the kind of text one would use to build an anthropological theory of Islam? Or what about this reason for 9/11 that Bin Laden gave to the world in his letter:

> You are the nation that permits Usury, which has been forbidden by all the religions. Yet you build your economy and investments on Usury. As a result of this, in all its different forms and guises, the Jews have taken control of your economy, through which they have taken control of your media, and now control all aspects of your life making you their servants and achieving their aims at your expense; precisely what Benjamin Franklin warned you against.[10]

One wonders if D'Souza missed these unhinged parts of bin Laden's letter, or whether he just decided to quote the lines that talked about "immorality" and "debauchery" and ignore the rhetorical backdrop of delusional anti-Semitic ramblings. In fact, what one reads in bin Laden's letter is no more a description of a Muslim view of American culture than Hitler's *Mein Kampf* was a macro-economics text book. Bin Laden's letter, like all his public statements, is a cowardly excuse for murder and a veiled threat of future genocide delivered in flowery nineteenth century rhetoric tinged with religious flair. It serves as a recruitment poster for future violence, not an ethnographic text for understanding culture. While it may be hard to imagine anyone who would read bin Laden's letter and use it as a primary source for building a political theory, D'Souza loses himself completely in the terrorist leader's violent mindset. After walking the reader through bin Laden's words, D'Souza no longer describes the left in America in political terms, but in the language of warfare and terrorism.

The transition is conscious on D'Souza's part and it is disturbing. He begins *The Enemy at Home* in a rhetorical frame that defines the left as an opposing set of politics seeking divergent cultural and policy goals from the right. By the end of the book, he has shifted the frame completely to define the left as an enemy insurgent force working in sync with the terrorists responsible for 9/11. In D'Souza's reading, the left fights U.S. forces in Iraq. The logic of his argument is somewhat convoluted, but the framing is clear. What makes the argument hard to navigate is the fact that D'Souza starts out by saying that bin Laden attacked the U.S. on 9/11 because of the cultural paganism of the left, but by the end of the book, he describes bin Laden and the left as working together to defeat U.S. forces in Iraq and achieve their supposedly shared goal of destroying George W. Bush. In D'Souza's reasoning, the Islamic fundamentalist once so outraged by homosexuality, usury and Jewish control of America switches to parroting the arguments of left-wing intellectuals in order to destroy the American barbarians. Likewise, the left that advocates freedom and emancipation for social groups most oppressed by Islamic fundamentalism becomes, in D'Souza's argument, a champion of Islamic fundamentalist terrorism. These twists of logic allow D'Souza to make the outrageous claim that the "enemy at home" has forged a multicultural alliance with the "axis of evil."

Here we jut up against the insidious aspect of D'Souza's logic. He is calculated in his use of military metaphors and descriptions of the left so that he sidesteps any literal accusation that the left is an actual armed and violent enemy. This rhetorical trick—denying the significance of the military metaphor—is the cognitive sleight of hand that lurks on every page of *The Enemy at Home*:

> The cultural left in this country is responsible for causing 9/11...In faulting the cultural left, I am not making the absurd claim that this group blew up the World Trade Center and the Pentagon[11]

> Conservatives need to expose the alliance between the left and Islamic radicals...I am not accusing anyone of treason or even anti-Americanism.[12]

Accusing someone through inference rather than direct statement is a cheap debating gimmick, and cowardly at that. Each time, D'Souza accuses the left of debauchery, ethnocentrism and collusion with terrorists, then quickly recants the charge in order to make a "cultural" argument about Islam's supposed hatred for America over liberal behavior and tastes. Despite his rhetorical acrobatics, D'Souza is by default accusing the left of high crimes.

The last chapter of the book is the most hypocritical and the most obvious in its intentions. After calling on conservatives to expose the cultural depravity of the left as the true enemy, D'Souza then recommends that conservatives open up a second front in the global war on terror. This front involves conservatives reaching out to moderate American, Middle-Eastern, and Central Asian Muslims with the purpose of working together to defeat fundamentalism abroad and liberalism at home.

Charges of "McCarthyism" have met D'Souza's call for a cultural purging of the American left. However, he denies that he is in any way engaging in that type of destructive politics, even though he concludes the book with a list of prominent people on the left who should be the first enemy targets of the second front of the war on terror. The implication is obvious and it is odious: The names that D'Souza provides are his recommendations for cultural purging. These are people who must be exposed not only for their responsibility in bringing about the death and destruction of 9/11, but for their role in preventing America from winning the global war on terror:

> If you presume that these individuals want Bush to win and bin Laden to lose the war on terror, their rhetoric and actions are utterly baffling. By contrast, if you presume that they want bin Laden to win and Bush to lose the war, then their statements and actions make perfect sense.[13]

The kind of conclusion that D'Souza goads his reader into drawing from the list is not about politics, but about crime. Specifically, he wants his readers to see the left as committing crimes against the state. The list he creates includes the names of every major liberal leader in Congress, academia, the Hollywood film industry, the Democratic Party, liberal think tanks, newspapers and non-profit organizations. As always, D'Souza describes this list of well-known leaders of American political, intellectual and cultural life in language lifted from a war crimes trial. At the same time, he never directly calls for the arrest or death of these leaders.

The juxtaposition of violent framing and the denial of direct accusation turns *The Enemy at Home* into a prolonged exercise in political misdirection. In specific terms, D'Souza introduces several violent concepts into the debate that muddy our understanding of national security, religion, and multiculturalism. Through a series of well-chosen quotes and suggestive references, D'Souza's hints that the current political debate in America is in fact a civil war, inviting his reader to embrace that logic. These are not hints designed to trick the reader. They are intellectual puzzles crafted to attract the attention of gifted readers, coaxing them into considering current party rifts to be sociological evidence of an insurmountable chasm that has opened up between left and right in America. Without actually branding the American left a new secessionist movement, D'Souza allows the keen reader to see the relationship between the last civil war and this supposed new one. The reader is then left to draw his or her own conclusion.

The first of D'Souza's strategic hints comes at the outset of the book , in an opening quote attributed baldly to Abraham Lincoln:

> Shall we expect some transatlantic military giant to step over the ocean and crush us at a blow? Never! All the armies of Europe, Asia and Africa combined, with all the treasure of the earth (our own excepted) in their military chest, with a Bonaparte for a commander, could not by force take a drink from the Ohio, or make a track on the Blue Ridge, in a trial of a thousand years. At what point, then, is the approach of danger to be expected? I answer, if it ever reach us, it must spring up amongst us. It cannot come from abroad. If destruction be our lot, we must ourselves be its author and finisher. As a nation of freemen, we must live through all time, or die by suicide.[14]

The message in this quote is plain enough, but the problem is the frame it creates for the chapters that follow. More than any other President, Abraham Lincoln symbolized the side of truth and justice in the American civil war—the side that stood firm against the threat to the union, and defeated it. The quote, thus, invites the reader to assume Lincoln's perspective as a departure point for understanding the causes of 9/11. This is a startling opening proposition.

Ironically, the Lincoln speech from which D'Souza quotes was an 1838 address called "The Perpetuation of Our Political Institutions," which Lincoln delivered while he was head of the Illinois Whig Party. The speech was not a warning about one side of American life threatening the other. Instead, Lincoln was lecturing on the importance of adhering to the rule of law instead of succumbing to violence. By taking the quote out of context and without attribution by date or location, D'Souza invites his readers to link his arguments about the American left as a "danger...among us" to Lincoln's struggle against the secessionist movement. In fact, Lincoln was very clear what "danger" he was talking about, qualifying it the very next line of the speech:

> I mean the increasing disregard for law which pervades the country; the growing disposition to substitute the wild and furious passions, in lieu of the sober judgment of Courts; and the worse than savage mobs, for the executive ministers of justice[15]

"Wild and furious passions" are, ironically, exactly what right-wing pundits try to force into American civic debate. Lincoln's speech developed a complex argument against this, suggesting that the experience of the American Revolution that had sustained our political institutions had begun to fade into distant memory. In Lincoln's estimation, this fading of the sustaining influence of the Revolution required that Americans renew their dedication to rational law and reason or else risk the collapse of the Republic into a form of violent anarchy. In many ways, the speech heralded Lincoln's broader devotion to deliberative democracy based on constitutionally defined political institutions. D'Souza uses Lincoln's quote to launch a theory of liberals as an "enemy at home." However, his theory runs directly counter to the actual meaning of the speech.

Despite this contradiction, D'Souza continues to drop hints that contemporary American politics is a new civil war, suggesting that the debate between Republicans and Democrats about 9/11 is somehow related to the debate over slavery that defined Lincoln's age. D'Souza's false parallel between the Civil War and current political debate is not his own invention, but a familiar theme used by many right-wing pundits. His innovation is to argue that Republicans and Democrats have reached the point where they no longer see each other as human beings:

> The vicious liberal attacks on Bush, which parallel the vicious conservative attacks on Clinton, are a way of saying, "We have difficulty recognizing you as human beings who inhabit the same moral planet that we do. Consequently we see you as usurpers and moral reprobates who should be hounded and driven from the corridors of power by any means necessary." [16]

The claim D'Souza presents is that the two political parties have reified each other as enemy objects worthy only of destruction. This is a mental view of enemy soldiers commonly found in young recruits who have just finished basic training and are en route to the front lines. By suggesting that Republicans and Democrats share this mind-set of dehumanizing the "enemy," and that the only question remaining is how to destroy "it," D'Souza sketches a scene ripe for civil war.

A far cry from the references to Lincoln and the cultural rift of the Civil War, D'Souza's most sinister arguments in *The Enemy at Home* come in his attempt to blame the prisoner abuses at Abu Ghraib on the "family values" of American liberals. D'Souza explains that the scandal at the Abu Ghraib prison was not about the violent sexual torture of prisoners by American forces, but about "sexual perversion" as distinct from violence. As Seymour Hersh explained in *The New Yorker* article that broke the scandal, however, what made the abuse at Abu Ghraib so horrific was not just the sexual violence of the abuses, but that the U.S. soldiers involved in the abuse photographed each other enjoying the suffering of the prisoners, seemingly as a form of memento:

> The photographs tell it all. In one, Private England, a ciga-
> rette dangling from her mouth, is giving a jaunty thumbs-
> up sign and pointing at the genitals of a young Iraqi, who
> is naked except for a sandbag over his head, as he mas-
> turbates. Three other hooded and naked Iraqi prisoners are
> shown, hands reflexively crossed over their genitals…Such
> dehumanization is unacceptable in any culture, but it is es-
> pecially so in the Arab world. Homosexual acts are against
> Islamic law and it is humiliating for men to be naked in
> front of other men.[17]

Despite Hersh's analysis, D'Souza claimed that liberal journalists downplayed not only the sexual aspect of the scandal, but also the impact it would have on traditional Muslim perceptions of American soldiers. Abu Ghraib, he claimed, was not a violent scandal, but an immoral sex scandal, a point he argued by recasting events into a narrative about irresponsible divorce turning into a pornographic military scandal:

> After marrying at age nineteen "on a whim," as she put it,
> England left her husband and enlisted in the military. There
> she met Graner, who was fresh from a divorce in which
> his wife had taken out three protective orders against him.
> Shortly before they went to Iraq, England and Graner par-
> tied together with another soldier friend in Virginia Beach.
> "They drank heavily," the *New York Times* reports, and when
> the other soldier passed out, "Private Graner and Private
> England took turns taking photographs of each other ex-
> posing themselves over his head." In Iraq, the two began an
> affair that they continued even though both were warned
> that their sexual trysts on the night shift violated military

rules. Soon Graner and England began to make videos of their sex acts. They circulated the videos among their friends, and even mailed some back to friends in America. In October 2004, Graner persuaded several other soldiers to join him in staging and photographing prisoners.[18]

After setting up the sexual exploits that followed England's and Graner's divorces, D'Souza then explains that "most Muslims did not view" the Abu Ghraib scandal as a "torture story," because they were already familiar with abuses under Saddam Hussein.[19] According to D'Souza:

> Abu Ghraib demonstrated the casualness with which married Americans have affairs, walk out on their spouses, and produce children without bothering to take responsibility for the care of the offspring.[20]

This manipulative reframing posits a situation so ludicrous that it would be comical if it were not set in the iconic military horror of the past decade. D'Souza would have us believe that when an Iraqi Muslim looked at the pictures from the scandal he did not see violence or torture, but divorce. D'Souza's argument is a strategic attempt to redefine Abu Ghraib as an example of the American liberal vices of divorce, single parenting, and sex out of wedlock exported to Iraq, where they manifested themselves as the perfect storm of promiscuity in the exploits of England and Graner. Beyond the sex, however, D'Souza explains that the shock perceived by Iraqi Muslims, and all Muslims by extension, was the threat of a liberal version of the nonpatriarchal family. According to D'Souza, the male-dominated family, the veil, and restrictive sexual mores are structures of authority and security in the Muslim world, and these structures are broadly perceived as threatened by the post-1950s egalitarian family. This threat fuels the flames of anger towards America. When liberals are not busy getting divorces and having irresponsible sex outside of marriage, D'Souza explains, they are criticizing traditional Muslim patriarchal families. Thus, he unveils liberals and their weak family values as a leading cause of the rise in global Muslim anger towards Americans in the wake of the Abu Ghraib scandal.

Lasciviousness brought on by divorce and single parenthood is just part of D'Souza's larger idea that an atheist crusade against Islam has caused terrorism:

> Radical Islam's most serious charge is that there is a war against Islam being waged by America, the fountainhead of atheism. It is this accusation—and this accusation alone— that explains why Muslims would fly planes into buildings or blow themselves up in suicide attacks against American targets.[21]

Somehow, D'Souza manages to locate a "war against" something as the cause for every social and political problem he considers. The question of religious conflict is no different. But here, again, he uses the idea of a war waged by the American left against Islam as a rhetorical tactic for separating liberalism out as the sole catalyst of global terrorism, and for reframing liberalism in violent terms as a secular crusade. D'Souza sees a United States that has become more secular over time, while the Muslim world has become more devout.[22] This is a wholly unconvincing claim given the explosive growth of mega-churches and religious participation in the past ten years. D'Souza's point, however, is not to get mired down in facts, but to build a case for the rise of secularism in America as a root cause for the growth of terrorism in the world. More secularism brought greater threat to Islam, which increased pressure for terrorists to wage the suicide attacks of September 11, 2001.

The problem, as D'Souza sees it, is not just the supposed decline in individual expressions of religious devotion, but an unholy separation of religion and politics in America's political institutions:

> No amount of surveys about the religious convictions of American people would convince Muslims, since this is not what Muslims mean when they charge that America is an atheist society. What they mean is that the public life of America—its government, laws, and policies—is intentionally divorced from religion.[23]

Just like Abu Ghraib, "divorce" is once again the problem. This time it is a divorce of God from politics brought on by the war waged by American liberals against religion. Why would American liberals wage such a war? The answer D'Souza provides once again brings in the question of violence. Liberals seek to destroy religion because they see religion as "the source of most of the division and violence throughout history."[24] Violence begets violence in D'Souza's inquisition of American liberals. By the end of the book, any clear debate on national security is consumed within his story of sexual perversity and liberal plotting.

The issue suppressed by violent language in the terrorism debate is "responsibility." The responsibility debate is about focusing the country on actions that produce real violence, versus pushing the logic of hidden threats that result in accusing half the American people of treason.

Ultimately, D'Souza's book takes a range of different topics in American and global politics and weaves them into a just-so story about the causes of violent mass murder. The end result is an argument that not only fails, but poisons any further discussion of the most important political question of our time: Who is responsible for 9/11? D'Souza would have us believe that the answer goes back to the hidden cultural threat of secular American liberalism, a theme that cuts across the work of many right-wing pundits. Islamic terrorists made the bombs and flew the planes into buildings, but the anti-religious left drove the terrorists to it by polluting the world with their divorces and intolerance. How convenient it is that this argument fits so perfectly into American two-party electoral politics. Since liberals are responsible for 9/11, D'Souza implicitly concludes, then you have to vote Republican. That conclusion is not only false, it is deeply cynical and fits into the broader effort by the Republican Party to argue that a vote for the Democrats is a vote for the terrorists. In other words, voting leads to violence.

But is there a better way to answer the question? If liberals are not responsible for 9/11, who is? The first step is remembering the direct answer to this question: Who did it? Before we get to questions of hidden threats, any discussion of 9/11 should begin with the people who committed the crimes. The same starting point also applies to Abu Ghraib: Who did it? This question takes the discussion through a very different logic than the argument about the hidden cultural threat.

In committing the attacks on September 11, 2001, the members of al Qaeda sought to use violence as a means of creating chaos and instability that would help them acquire global power. Starting with the practical description of events, we should hold responsible those who committed the crimes. The nature of the crimes committed on 9/11, thus, brings the question of responsibility to a vexing place because all the people directly responsible for the crimes ended up killing themselves in the act of committing the crime. To hold people accountable, therefore, we must expand our definition along a chain of responsibility that includes not just those who directly committed the acts of murder, but also those who helped plan and fund those acts.

By framing responsibility in terms of "chains" anchored in the violent act, and connecting the act to the people responsible for the violence, we can begin to sketch out appropriate responses. Thinking of 9/11 in terms of a chain of responsibility is very different than thinking in terms of hidden threats. Following chains of responsibility, we avoid leaping to an ideological argument and stay grounded in people and actions. Moreover, thinking in terms of hidden enemies buried within our own society creates a political dynamic fueled by paranoia and suspicion, and leads people to see the surface of politics—the surface of their everyday lives—as a mere smokescreen to the dangerous reality beneath.

In the case of 9/11, the difficult reality Americans faced went far beyond the violence of the murder of thousands of innocent people. As a nation, the attacks on 9/11 symbolized an end to decades of assumed safety and security at home, which left Americans confused and concerned. While some in government understood the possibility of people using commercial airplanes to attack office buildings, most citizens had never considered this possibility. Hence, while we watched the events unfold on TV in excruciating detail, we also began to doubt that as a nation we were prepared to protect ourselves from this new kind of sudden and unexpected violence. Even with the entire history of American military might in our heads, nothing seemed adequate to reassure us that we would be safe.

In that environment, most Americans immediately began thinking in terms of chains of responsibility, ultimately leading to widespread support for the invasion of Afghanistan. Beyond bin Laden and his al Qaeda organization, the American public saw that the chain of responsibility extended to the Taliban. The next logical step should have been to continue pursuing that chain of responsibility—to seize bin Laden and bring him to trial, and to continue to push further and further along the chain until the fullest extent of the criminal acts had been prosecuted. Along the way, we would have developed legal means to be more effective at monitoring such acts as they were taking shape by increasing the legal surveillance system, growing international security networks, strengthening alliances, and developing technological innovations to help stay connected with international partners and interrupt criminal networks before they gave rise to another attack.

Instead of that approach, the Bush administration chose to switch the public debate to the logic of hidden threats by arguing that al Qaeda was not a network of individuals linked through a chain of responsibility, but an evil force lurking beneath the surface of all nations hostile to American interests. In this vein, the purpose of our military was to root out al Qaeda so that it could not produce another 9/11. Years later, long after the actions of the Iraq invasion continued to produce more violence, the Bush administration and the Republican Party pushed the logic of hidden threats, clinging to the idea that the only way to avoid a future attack as bad or worse than the attacks of 9/11 was to destroy the hidden threat. Therein lies the madness. For if the actual destruction of the hidden threat is revealed, then other hidden threats will become even more hidden before they can be found. And so, the logic of hidden threats leads to a radical form of government sponsored secret violence based on the idea that only a hidden cure can defeat a hidden threat. As that logic spread in post-9/11 America, so did the idea that the protection of civil liberties stood in the way of protecting the country from future attacks. Concern for civil liberties, after all, is fundamentally about casting light on abuses of the Bill of Rights. To bring anything to light about the "hunt" for hidden terrorists was in and of itself deemed to be a danger.

In the case of the horrific incidents at Abu Ghraib, the public saw first and foremost how this logic transformed America into a type of anachronistic brutality. And yet, the widespread acceptance of the idea that torture was the only path to safety was actually far worse than the photographs of cruelty that came to light in the Abu Ghraib scandal. Long after the photos of hooded and abused Iraqi prisoners circulated in the media, the emergence of water boarding as a chosen technique amongst interrogators surfaced. In late 2007, former CIA officer John Kiriakou voiced the twisted logic of hidden threats that made him decide to torture a prisoner named Abu Zubaydah:

> The decision was made because he was so wholly uncooperative. It went for weeks and weeks where he just wouldn't answer any questions, wouldn't cooperate at all. And we

were certain that he had important information that we could use to foil future al Qaeda attacks...The next day he told his interrogator that Allah had visited him in his cell during the night and told him to cooperate because it would make it easier on the other brothers who had been captured.[25]

While the CNN interviewer, John Roberts, asked a variety of questions about the technique of waterboarding used in this and in many other similar instances, he never asked Kiriakou two obvious questions. First, why would a man who is willing to turn his own suicide and the suicide of his charges into a weapon against the United States worry about discomfort or death in an American prison? Abu Zubaydah was responsible for convincing young men to hop on a plane and obliterate themselves by crashing into buildings. But in less than a day, he became concerned that they might experience some physical discomfort during interrogation? Roberts could have asked that question, but did not.

The second question Roberts did not ask was: How was a CIA agent "certain" about information which was supposedly hidden within a suspect's mind? It is worth pausing to consider the twisted logic that Kiriakou unfolded for CNN viewers, which falls somewhere in between a Kafka short story and a scene from Orwell's *1984*. Despite the fact that the CIA did not know what Abu Zubaydah knew, they, nonetheless, knew for certain that what he knew was what they needed to know. In other words: The CIA officers' ignorance made them certain that the torture of this man would end their ignorance. In essence, a former government employee appeared on TV and boldly claimed that he had broken the law, but that breaking the law was just a one-off, temporary glitch in a desperate moment and that the danger of further attacks disappeared as a result of waterboarding Abu Zubaydah. It is clear, however, that what vanished in that interrogation room was not the ignorance of the CIA officers or the threat of future attacks. What dissipated like mist that day was Kiriakou's responsibility to uphold the United States Constitution, to honor the trust of the American people, and to defend a system of laws. Absolute authority rooted in fear took their place. In that new environment, the "certainty" that drove Kiriakou and his CIA colleagues to choose torture found its way far beyond the confines of the interrogation room. Suddenly, danger was hidden everywhere.

D'Souza's argument in *The Enemy at Home* extends the logic of hidden threats to the ongoing political discussion about culture, thereby redefining American liberals as treasonous. This is misguided. Focusing the debate on responsibility instead of hidden threats would not only have expanded the sense of national unity following the attacks, but would have also pushed Americans to action instead of suspicion.

9. THE RETURN OF PRAGMATISM

Some may brush aside a study of the right-wing punditry's impact on American democracy as too one-sided, raising alarm that the purpose of such a book is political, not analytical, inflammatory, not productive. With these two concerns in mind, I offer two explanations.

First, this book is not intended as an ideological statement, but as an attempt to bring the debate on violence in American politics up to date. In this respect, *Outright Barbarous* is a follow up to Hannah Arendt's landmark study *On Violence*, written over forty years ago. Despite her general focus on the question of violence, Arendt also wrote a relatively one-sided book in that she analyzed the way violence framed left-wing politics. She did so, however, not by ideological prejudice, but in response to the political context of her time. The same is true here. Arendt's book is poignant because it moves beyond critique to offer a general model for how to study violence in politics. Violence, she teaches us, is not only a description of a kind of destructive action, but also a way of thinking and speaking. To understand what violence is in politics, she argued, we must first figure out how people are discussing it amongst themselves. Thus, to understand why many of the protest movements of the 1960s espoused violence, Arendt analyzed the ideas about violence that were "in the air" at the time, particularly the works of European intellectuals Georges Sorel, Franz Fanon, and Jean Paul-Sartre.[1] Arendt explained that the ideas of those prominent writers convinced followers of the 1960s political movements that violence was the only path to power and that the outcomes of violence could be controlled. The intellectuals were wrong, Arendt explained, as the outcomes of violence are always uncertain and are a byproduct of social change, not the engine that drives it. She thus concluded that the left-wing protest movements of the 1960s that embraced violence were actually working against their own interests by creating opportunities for entrenched political groups to step in and exert political control in moments of uncertainty. For readers seeking to balance my analysis of the right-wing with an analysis of the left, Arendt's book offers the best starting point.

Second, my focus on violent language is not just borne out of an interest in right-wing writing or speaking—although that is certainly a motivating factor—but, rather, my expression of concern for a growing trend in American politics. As such, this book is intended as a cautionary tale for elected officials and candidates in institutional politics as much as a study of political pundits in the broadcast media. There are many instances where contemporary politicians use violent language to frame contemporary elections and policy debates. Newt Gingrich, for example, brings violence into the first pages of his latest political manifesto, *America Winning the Future: A 21st Century Contract With America*. The similarities between Gingrich's words and the words of the right-wing pundits who dominate the airwaves are astounding. Just as those writers have done in their books and TV appearances, Gingrich frames his discussion of his political agenda with the violence of 9/11:

> Imagine the morning after an attack even more devastating than 9/11. The threats are real and could literally destroy our country. There are weapons of mass destruction, weapons

of mass murder, and weapons of mass disruption—nuclear is first, biological and chemical is second, electromagnetic pulse (EMP) is third. All are real, and we are lulled into complacency by the fact that none is currently being used.[2]

Previously, Gingrich's political rhetoric was framed by a logic of social and economic "contracts," wherein he invited the American public to view themselves as signers of a social compact with the Republican Party. Since 9/11, Gingrich's mindset has changed. While his agenda for America still bears traces of the logic of "contracts," Gingrich has front-loaded the new version with hypothetical scenarios of America's fiery demise. He has become a voice of the violent right.

Similarly, former New York mayor Rudolph Giuliani brings violence into his vision for America as outlined in his book *Leadership*. Ostensibly a manual on what constitutes the best leadership skills, Giuliani's entire narrative is framed by the fiery violence of a terrorist attack:

> Then the second plane hit. All I saw was a big flash of fire. By that point we were at Canal Street, which marks the beginning of Manhattan's southern tip. Initially, I thought it was the first tower experiencing a secondary explosion, but Patti got a call from Police Command saying the south tower, Tower 2, had also been struck, by what turned out to be United Airlines Flight 175, a 767 en route from Boston to LA. This convinced us it was terrorism.[3]

Giuliani devotes most of his book to autobiographical episodes in which he offers his own pugnacity, loyalty, and persistence as evidence of leadership. The narrative as a whole, however, is framed by the violent idea that his leadership abilities were steeled by the fires of 9/11. As Giuliani's campaign collapsed and John McCain rose up to claim the Republican nomination, the initial violent framing shifted from the recent violence of 9/11 to the historic violence of World War II. In the paean to his leadership qualities, which took the form of a March 2008 YouTube viral-video-cum-campaign-ad titled "Man in the Arena," McCain cast himself as the cosmic heir to Winston Churchill's refusal to surrender to violent foes, skipping past the single day of violence that weighed most on America's memory—September 11, 2001—to reframe the election as the Battle of Britain. Dutifully stepping up to re-enforce this message, the Republican noise machine used McCain's framing to maintain the sturdy bridge between right-wing politics and the media.

It would be wrong, however, to conclude from these observations that the solution to violent language from right-wing pundits and politicians is to find a way to control speech in America. Beyond the general principles of free speech as defined by our Constitution and discussed in the beginning of this book, a broad push for more stringent controls would be counterproductive. The answer is not to take people's words away from them, but to shift the debate itself. To do that will require two very basic, but important steps. First, we need to understand why free and open conversation is the core foundation of American democracy and how those conversations work. Second, we need to find innovative ways to stimulate and protect that foundation. Ultimately, violent language poisons our democracy not because it is unpleasant to hear or read, but because it shuts down the deliberative process itself. And it is that deliberative process that we must reclaim, revive, and champion.

A "deliberative" democracy is a political system marked by a very distinct form of participation. In such a system, consensus is not imposed by rule of force, but emerges as a result of people participating in many different kinds of open, inclusive, and rational conversations.[4] Some of these conversations are in government or town hall meetings, while others take place in the informal settings of our everyday lives, such as coffee shops, carpools, or at the dinner table.[5] Most of us do not even think about this aspect of American society because it not only functions well in our system, but it also functions without considerable effort from us on a daily basis.

The key to understanding the power of a deliberative system is to contrast it with what it is not. For example, prior to the American Revolution, the colonists lived in a monarchical system, where the king ruled by imposing his will on the people. What is missing in a tyrannical monarchy is not just an elected government, but the practice of citizens gathering together to discuss ideas, reach consensus, and then apply the fruits of those conversations to the decisions of government.

Another system different from deliberative democracy is a participatory democracy. In a participatory system, decisions are imposed by the will of the majority. Unlike a deliberative democracy, where a lone person with a persuasive argument can have influence, in a participatory system, power is all about numbers. In such a system, a tyranny of the majority can emerge in horrific ways. Often when people talk about the need for greater participation in American political life, they mistakenly refer to that as "participatory democracy," when they are really calling for more participation in the deliberative process.[6]

When we talk about deliberative democracy, therefore, we mean a system where the people express their opinions via conversation, and then that opinion circulates both in the media and through political institutions for the benefit of good governance. As sociologist Jürgen Habermas explains, the deliberative aspect of our democracy took shape a half century before the American Revolution, when through conversations about politics and social life in the coffee houses of England and the salons of France, a new "public sphere" emerged.[7] But the public sphere facilitated more than just chats over coffee; it was also connected to the emergence of a new kind of media that was ideal for capturing and circulating public opinion: newspapers. Habermas argues that these public conversations about politics, amplified and circulated by the media, ultimately gave rise to the shape and content of deliberative debate and became the basic practice at the heart of all democratic governments.[8]

Unfortunately, as Habermas laments, the public sphere has weakened since it first came into being, a change he attributes to a lost passion for discussion in politics and the rise of a mass media with entertainment for profit as its central goal.[9] As influential and important as the deliberations of the public sphere are, they depend on a public interested in discussing issues of political and social importance. Moreover, the public sphere also depends on a media with an interest in that conversation that is prioritized above its bottom line. When the public is no longer driven to discuss politics, and the media becomes a vehicle for circulating entertainment, the conversation deteriorates.

Healthy or unhealthy as it may be in a given historical moment, deliberative democracy can only withstand so much violent language before it buckles and collapses. Overly confrontational and violent rhetoric can stimulate debate and opinion up to a point, but it scuttles deliberation if overused. Too much violent language gums up the debate by replacing the level-headed exchange of ideas with sensationalism. More than just a tone or style, sensationalism grows out of the way that right-wing pundits frame political issues. Constant talk of murder, treason, gunshots, and terrorism whip up the emotions and pulls people's attention away from analytical thinking. Public engagement becomes passive observation, participants become audiences, and conversation becomes entertainment. As John Dewey observed, sensationalism shuts down our curiosity about the relationship between things by overwhelming us with a focus on raw, isolated, and shocking events.[10] By contrast, too much cool rationality can also be a detriment to deliberative conversation. Imagine talking politics with someone who never raised their voice—the result would be sleep inducing! The key to healthy deliberative conversation is striking a productive balance between passion and rationality.[11]

Violence is the opposite of conversation, and as such, the antithesis of the kind of participation that defines our deliberative system. This distinction is so fundamental to being American that we all learn to view violence as the opposite of deliberation throughout our schooling. Reading books like George Orwell's *1984*, studying the history of Nazi Germany, and watching films about the Civil Rights movement in the South not only teaches us about tyranny, injustice, and oppression, but also help us to understand that a democracy is healthy when people are able to gather and talk rationally about political challenges. We also learn that violent language becomes the norm in systems that advance anti-democratic ideologies; eventually in these anti-democratic contexts, the public square collapses into an arena of public humiliation, exclusion, and discrimination. Likewise, we also learn from a young age that the return to deliberative democracy brings with it the restoration of the public sphere, and government, as a place for the free, open, and rational exchange of ideas. Instilling this awareness of and faith in deliberative conversation is one of the core lessons that prepares students to take on the responsibilities of citizenship.

In light of how dependent our democratic system is on free and open debate, finding productive ways to move beyond the sensationalism of violent language presents a challenge to political journalism, our system of education, and the media industry. To avoid unproductive calls for the censorship of violent language, we must pursue key innovations in writing, media, and public life. Following the example of George Orwell's "six rules" for overcoming the problems of political language, I propose the following six suggestions to resolve the problem of violent language in the American political media:

I. Stop using "war" metaphors.
II. Revive expository journalism.
III. Invest in local media.
IV. Increase citizen participation.
V. Introduce a rating system for political entertainment.
VI. Create new deliberative forums.

These suggestions include more than the rules about writing style as proposed by Orwell because the problem of violent language extends past writing to include government and society. While it is important for journalists to recognize the value of choosing not to frame current events with violence, equally important roles must be played both by government and individuals.

Without trying to limit the speech of others, journalists can commit themselves to reporting the news without using a "war" metaphor to frame ideas. The problem with describing every political episode as a "war on [blank]" is not just the inherent violence, but the vagueness. Likewise, elected officials and policy makers can also reject the impulse to frame every initiative as a "war on" something. As important as it has been in the past to rally Americans to work for the public good by seeing themselves as soldiers in a war against a given problem, the time has come to diversify the metaphors we use. Talking about policy in terms other than "war" may seem strange to many people at first, given the virtual monopoly that the "war" logic holds on our way of thinking at the moment. How do we move past this?

In my first book, *Framing the Debate,* I suggested that reading great speeches from past U.S. Presidents was a good way of adding new options to our rhetorical toolkit. Franklin Roosevelt and Lyndon Johnson, for example, presented some of the most challenging policy initiatives in U.S. history by using "safety net" and "building" metaphors. Proposing to decrease poverty in old age and restore balance to the national economy, Roosevelt framed a government pension program as a form of "social'" insurance that would be available to everyone in times of need. To this day, most Americans understand social security in those terms and feel a sense of concern whenever politicians propose taking that safety net away. Several decades later, Johnson framed a wide range of policies to improve schools, the environment, and urban centers through the architectural metaphor of "building" a great society. This metaphor helped the public see the multiple steps that went into reviving the nation and provided a multitude of avenues for citizens to contribute their efforts and idealism. Forty years later, a majority of Americans still dedicate their lives to building Johnson's Great Society.

It will take a leap of faith for many journalists and politicians to step away from violent metaphors. But as Orwell wrote, the first rule of fighting vagueness in political language is to "never use a metaphor, simile or other figure of speech which you are used to seeing in print."[12] Perhaps someday, "war" and other violent metaphors will become so underused in American political debate that they will again be useful for presenting ideas clearly. For now, it is time to let them go.

Regaining the great American tradition of expository journalism is an essential step towards diminishing the impact of violent language and, ultimately, restoring the public sphere. Expository writing seeks to describe events and phenomena in order to explain how something works. While typically written in the third person, it need not be. It is, however, the counterweight to polemical writing, wherein the author presents opinion in order to persuade the reader. The great power of expository writing comes from the writer's ability to focus the reader on facts and details, as well as the relationship between them. In contrast to the shock of violent polemic, expository writing inspires the reader to think in terms of the relationship between facts, as well as cause and effect—the basic building blocks of a deliberative debate.

Muckraking journalism in the early twentieth century was an expository movement. Whereas the Muckrakers knew that many large corporations and trusts of their day were engaged in unjust practices that caused harm to ordinary people, they recognized that the public did not understand the basic workings of these companies enough to see the point. Books like Upton Sinclair's *The Jungle* were powerful because they allowed people to see for the first time how factory production lead to the physical, economic, and social harm of workers. Sinclair and his cohorts had strong beliefs about social justice, but their journalism was driven by the power of expository writing. Reducing the impact of contemporary right-wing pundits will require a similar commitment to socially minded expository journalism by a new generation of writers.

Violent rhetoric is a product of national pundits who often have no connection to or responsibility for local communities. By combining nationally syndicated columns with nationally broadcast TV spots, pundits pushing violent frames dominate the media market at multiple levels. What is rarely talked about, however, is how their rhetoric undermines and undervalues local media and broadcasting. Even though local media reports on events of much greater relevance to people's daily lives, the business of local reporting and broadcasting has been in financial crisis for years. The decline of local media has been devastating for deliberative conversations on municipal and state level political issues.

Restoring a local focus to media is a crucial step to protecting deliberative debate from violent rhetoric, but the solution requires more than just making the choice to watch local broadcasts and read local journalism. The private sector and the public sector must both invest in local media. Moreover, federal limits on media ownership must be enforced to prevent more cost-effective national syndication from displacing local programming. Still, the investment in local media will be ineffective if individuals do not make the choice to return to the regular habit of viewing local media. Despite the familiar axiom that "all politics is local," it has become difficult to focus public attention on local political media. One way to garner attention is for local media to insist on playing a greater role in events of national interest. All events in a presidential election season, for example, take place in some local context, but are usually run by national broadcasting. Local media could play a greater role by insisting on hosting debates, televised town hall meetings, and major speeches. Local news teams could also insist on playing a greater role in political analysis, thereby, breaking the monopoly national pundits often hold on this influential kind of broadcasting. The challenge is not insurmountable, but it will take time, investment, and persistence to restore public faith and interest in local media.

Violent language has the power to dominate politics because national pundits enjoy a monopoly power on public opinion. One of the most effective ways to overcome that monopoly is public participation in the media. Despite the millions of bloggers who now contribute to political media on the Internet, participation by the public is relatively small. The solution is to encourage people to participate in the political media by launching a series of public awareness programs. This initiative would be similar to the public awareness campaigns that promoted knowledge of the environment, civics, drug abuse, and smoking in the 1970s, 1980s, and 1990s.

New media technology presents an unprecedented opportunity for citizens to dilute the impact of violent language on the national debate. Twenty years ago, the highest level of participation an engaged citizen could have in the daily news cycle was through the writing of a letter to the editor. Today, however, citizens with a rudimentary knowledge of computers can post their own TV broadcasts for relatively little cost. Government must play an active role in promoting greater citizen participation in new media with the goal of bringing more and more people into the deliberative conversation.

American viewers have not been well served by the obsolete TV ratings system currently in place. While the system does offer adequate help to parents seeking to evaluate shows for adult content, it fails to address the entertainment aspect of many political shows. Private cable channels, such as HBO, have taken the initiative by making sure that even political entertainment (e.g., *Real Time With Bill Maher*) include ratings warnings at the start of each show—a welcome practice. Broadcast networks and cable stations dedicated to news, however, have not followed this lead, despite the fact that some of their programming mixes politics and entertainment.

The solution to this problem starts with the Federal Communications Commission convening a study that analyzes and defines political entertainment, and then proposes ways to devise an appropriate system of ratings. The FCC can then actively promote the use of such a content ratings system for entertainment oriented political shows that consistently include violent language, themes, and ideas. Just as a rating screen appears prior to a film or series with adult content, a ratings screen could appear prior to the start of political entertainment. If the show regularly includes violent language, for example, the viewer would, thus, have an opportunity to learn that through the ratings system. The goal would not be to limit speech, but to provide the viewer with a resource they can use to decide if a political entertainment show is something they wish to watch—or allow their children to view.

Because violent language weakens the foundation of deliberative democracy, strengthening our system also requires the creation of new opportunities for deliberative conversation. During the 2007/2008 presidential primary season, the public witnessed exactly this kind of innovation: candidate forums. Whereas such forums had been few and far between in past primary seasons, their number suddenly increased dramatically, a powerful sign of how dedicated the American public remains to increasing the vibrancy of the public sphere and of maintaining the channels of deliberative conversation between citizens and elected officials.

These forums had the effect of momentarily reviving the public sphere by mediating conversations about politics over great distances. In addition, new media, such as YouTube, were then able to preserve the fruits of those deliberations, circulate them widely, and bring them to the attention of the people serving in government. The overwhelming success of these election-oriented candidate events suggests there would also be interest in new deliberative forums beyond the campaign season. Ideally, deliberative forums could take place throughout the year at both the local and national level.

THE RISE OF THE PRAGMATIC PUNDIT

How long it will take to turn back the tide of violent language is difficult to estimate. While Americans express both shock and fatigue in response to the violent language of right-wing pundits, the ability of the punditry to generate profits for media companies means that there will be a sizeable counterweight against any attempt to resolve the problem. And it is not easy at first for individuals to commit themselves to participate in and take responsibility for deliberative democracy. Not everyone has enough time or energy.

Over time, however, pushing back against violent rhetoric from right-wing pundits will result in a fundamental shift from violence to pragmatism in our experience of politics and media. In particular, as the sun sets on pundits who use violent frames, a new generation of pragmatic pundits will step up to take their place. As American philosopher William James suggested, pragmatism is distinguished by a broad concern for "practical consequences" or "what difference would it practically make if this notion or that notion were true?"[13] Unlike pundits who frame issues in violent language, the overriding concern of a pragmatic pundit is to make sure their presentation helps the reader understand actual consequences without reference to ideology. If it helps explain practical consequences, the pragmatic pundit will not shy away from violent metaphors or frames. Yet, the pragmatic pundit begins with the recognition that violence is very helpful at a practical level only in the most extreme and rare circumstances.

Consider the global climate debate. At first, the challenge of finding a way to lower the level of carbon pollution seems best described in violent terms. To end the climate crisis, we must fight a "Global War on Global Warming."[14] On second thought, however, a pragmatic pundit sees how a violent frame contradicts the pragmatics of protecting the environment. Our goal is to burn less carbon resources, to clean up air pollution, to grow food in ways that sustain our fields, and to invent technologies that harness renewable energy. And the goal of the climate debate is not just to find the best ways to accomplish these goals, but to act so that our children inherit a world in better shape than the world left to us. Conservation is those combined acts of building, inventing, sustaining and inheriting. To frame the debate as a "war" of conservation is confusing and impractical. We reach for "war" in this instance not because it helps us achieve our common goals, but out of habit. The pragmatic pundit recognizes the problems in the violent frame and gets to work providing better description and clearer explanation.

Consider the debate about the economy. At first, it may seem that the struggle to restore economic justice in America is best discussed in a violent frame. In his recent book, conservative libertarian pundit Lou Dobbs describes the economy as a "war" on America's middle class.[15] Pausing for a moment, the pragmatic pundit recognizes that a violent frame runs counter to the practical goals of the discussion. "Every working man and woman in this country must fight back against the powerful forces," Dobbs tells his reader. Those forces are "political, economic, and social" and they "threaten our way of life."[16] Rather than inspire people to participate in local government and revive deliberative democracy, Dobbs' call to "war" has led people to see the American government as a hostile enemy. It has also rallied people to see immigration as an alien "invasion." To restore the U.S. economy, we must protect jobs, revive local industries, uphold fair labor standards, and negotiate fairer agreements with foreign governments. The pragmatic pundit recognizes that violent rhetoric hinders the debate and looks for new ways to bring understanding to the practical challenges at hand.

Consider the debate about civil liberties. To some, it seemed necessary following the attacks of 9/11 to reframe the United States Constitution through the lens of "war." In his book *War By Other Means: An Insider's Account of the War on Terror,* former Assistant Attorney General John Yoo redefined the Constitution as a document protecting the president's power to fight terrorism. By doing so, Yoo claimed through a legalistic argument that in the wake of 9/11, the president's unitary power as defined by the Constitution was limitless. "The power to protect the nation," Yoo wrote, attributing the thought to Alexander Hamilton, "ought to exist without limitation."[17] On closer inspection, the pragmatic pundit realizes that 9/11 created confusion on this issue, and looks for new and better ways to describe and explain it.

We cannot, as Orwell warned, "change this all in a moment." The violent language of right-wing pundits will not dissipate as a result of mere exposure to critical analysis. But we can change one political debate at a time with the simple act of making new choices about how to write and speak. As our habit of using violent language wanes, a pragmatic habit will begin to take its place. This new pragmatism will help guide us towards deliberative conversation, while the right-wing tactic of using violent language will tarnish and fade.

SELECTED REFERENCES

Adorno, Theodore. *The Authoritarian Personality*. New York: Harper, 1950.

Arendt, Hannah. *On Revolution*. New York: Penguin Books, 1963.

Arendt, Hannah. *On Violence*. New York: Harcourt Brace & Company, 1969.

Brown, Sherrod. *Myths of Free Trade: Why American Trade Policy Has Failed*. New York: New Press, 2004.

Buchanan, Patrick. *Death Of The West*. New York: St. Martin's Press, 2002.

Choate, Pat. *Agents of Influence*. New York: Simon & Schuster, 1990.

Clausewitz, Carl von. *On War*. New York: Oxford University Press, 2007.

Coulter, Ann. *Treason: Liberal Treachery From the Cold War to the War On Terrorism*. New York: Crown Forum, 2003.

D'Souza, Dinesh. *Letters To A Young Conservative*. New York: Basic Books, 2002.

D'Souza, Dinesh. *The Enemy at Home*. New York: Doubleday, 2007.

Dewey, John. *The Political Writings*. Indianapolis: Hackett Publishing, 1993.

Dobbs, Lou. *The War on the Middle Class: How the Government, Big Business, and Special Interest Groups Are Waging War on the American Dream and How to Fight Back*. New York: Viking, 2007.

Dobson, James. *Marriage Under Fire: Why We Must Win This Battle*.

Carol Stream, IL: Tyndale House Publishers, 2007.

Dobson, James. *Bringing Up Boys*. Carol Stream, IL: Tyndale House Publishers, 2001.

Dobson, James. *Dare To Discipline*. Carol Stream, IL: Tyndale House Publishers, 1992.

Federal Communications Commission. *Violent Programming And Its Impact In Children*. April 6, 2007, FCC 07-50, MB Docket No. 04-261.

Feldman, Jeffrey. *Framing the Debate: Famous Presidential Speeches and How Progressives Can Use Them To Change the Conversation and Win Elections*. New York: Ig Publishing, 2007.

Filler, Lewis. *The Muckrakers*. Stanford: Stanford University Press, 1968.

Gibson, John. *The War On Christmas: How The Liberal Plot To Ban The Sacred Christian Holiday Is Worse Than You Thought*. New York: Sentinal, 2005.

Gingrich, Newt. *Winning the Future: A 21st Century Contract With America*. Washington, DC: Regnery Publishing, Inc., 2006.

Giuliani, Rudolph. *Leadership*. New York: Hyperion, 2002.

Gore, Al. *The Assault On Reason*. New York: The Penguin Press, 2007.

Gore, Al. *An Inconvenient Truth: The Planetary Emergency of Global Warming and What We Can Do About It*. New York: Rodale Books, 2006.

Isikoff, Michael. *Uncovering Clinton: A Reporter's Story*. New York, Three Rivers Press, 1999.

James, William. *Pragmatism: A New Way For Some Old Ways Of Thinking*. New York: Longmans, Green and Co., 1907.

Lakoff, George. *Whose Freedom? The Battle Over America's Most Important Idea*. New York: Picador, 2007.

LaPierre, Wayne. *Guns, Freedom and Terrorism*. Nashville: WND Books, 2003.

Naomi Klein. *The Shock Doctrine: The Rise of Disaster Capitalism*. New York: Metropolitan Books, 2007.

O'Reilly, Bill. *Culture Warrior.* New York: Broadway, 2006.

Orwell, George. *Why I Write.* New York: Penguin Books, 1984.

Rorty, Richard. *Achieving Our Country: Leftist Thought in Twentieth-Century America.* Cambridge: Harvard University Press, 1998.

Sirota, David. *Hostile Takeover: How Big Money And Corruption Conquered Our Government—And How We Take It Back.* New York: Crown, 2006.

Tocqueville, Alexis de. *Democracy in America,* ed. J.P. Maier, trans. George Lawrence, Garden City, N.Y.: Anchor Books, 1969

Tse-Tung, Mao. *Quotations From Chairman Mao-Tse Tung.* China Books and Periodicals, Inc., 1990.

Weber, Max. *Political Writings.* Cambridge: Cambridge University Press, 1994.

Williams, Raymond. *Keywords: A Vocabulary of Culture and Society.* New York: Oxford University Press, 1976.

NOTES

Preface

1. Clara Jeffrey, "NRA's Response To Virginia Tech Shootings: Stand Your Ground," *Mother Jones*, April 16, 2007, http://www.motherjones.com/mojoblog/archives/2007/04/4194_nras_response_t.html.

2. "Thanks for staying with us. I'm Bill O'Reilly. In "The Factor" follow up segment tonight, as we said in the "Talking Points Memo", it was only minutes, minutes before the far left in America began turning the Virginia Tech murders into an anti-gun story." Bill O'Reilly, *The O'Reilly Factor*, April 17, 2007.

3. Ann Coulter, "Let's Make America A 'Sad Free Zone'!" April 18, 2007, http://www.anncoulter.com/cgi-local/article.cgi?article=179.

4. E. J. Dionne, Jr., "Gun Law Pragmatism," *The Washington Post*, April 20, 2007, A31.

5. Jeffrey Feldman, *Framing the Debate: Famous Presidential Speeches and How Progressives Can Use Them To Change the Conversation and Win Elections*, (New York: Ig Publishing, 2007), 71-72.

6. Lyndon Johnson, "Annual Message To The Congress On The State Of The Union," January 8, 1964. For a full text of this speech see, The American Presidency Project, http://www.presidency.ucsb.edu/ws/?pid=26787.

7. "We must quickly mobilize our civilization with the urgency and resolve that has previously been seen only when nations mobilized for war." For full text of speech see, "Speech by Al Gore On the Acceptance of the Nobel Peace Prize," Oslo, Norway," *The Huffington Post*, December 10, 2007, http://www.huffingtonpost.com/2007/12/10/read-al-gores-nobel-priz_n_76054.html.

8. Al Gore, *The Assault On Reason* (New York: The Penguin Press), 2007.

1. Violent Right

1. George Orwell, *Why I Write* (New York: Penguin Books, 1984) 102.

2. Orwell 116.

3. Orwell 117.

4. Orwell 119.

5. Hannah Arendt, *On Violence* (New York: Harcourt Brace & Company, 1969).

6. Mao Tse-Tung, "Problems of War and Strategy" (1938). Cited in *Quotations From Chairman Mao-Tse Tung* (China Books and Periodicals, Inc., 1990), 61.

7. "For the purpose of our deliberations I wish only to establish the purely conceptual ground as follows: the modern state is an institutional association of rule (Herrschaftsverband) which has successfully established the monopoly of physical violence as a means of rule within a territory." Max Weber, *Political Writings* (Cambridge: Cambridge University Press, 1994), 316.

8. George W. Bush, "Remarks of the President at the Pentagon," September 17, 2001, http://www.whitehouse.gov/news/releases/2001/09/20010917-3.html.

9. See "Statement of Principles," Project For The New American Century, June 3, 1997, http://www.newamericancentury.org/statementofprinciples.htm.

10. Pat Robertson interview with Jerry Falwell, *The 700 Club*, September 13, 2001, http://www.commondreams.org/news2001/0917-03.htm.

11. Mark Lacey, "N.R.A. Stands By Criticism Of President," *The New York Times*, March 20, 2000, A:18.

12. Richard Cheney, "Vice President and Mrs. Cheney's Remarks and Q&A at a Town Hall Meeting," September 7, 2004, http://www.

whitehouse.gov/news/releases/2004/09/20040907-8.html.

13. West Virginia State Board of Education et al. v. Barnette et al, 319 U.S. 624, 63 S.Ct. 1178 (1943).

14. Federal Communications Commission, *Violent Programming And Its Impact In Children*, April 6, 2007, FCC 07-50, MB Docket No. 04-261.

2. The War On Guns

1. Wayne LaPierre, "Frightened, Or Free," Speech Given by NRA Executive Vice President Wayne LaPierre to The Conservative Political Conference, Arlington, VA, February 1, 2001, http://www.nra.org/Speech.aspx?id=6031.

2. Wayne LaPierre interviewed by Sean Hannity and Alan Colmes, *Hannity & Colmes*, March 225, 2002.

3. For a fascinating perspective on how right-wing pundits understand the word 'freedom,' see George Lakoff, *Whose Freedom? The Battle Over America's Most Important Idea* (New York: Picador, 2007), 95-110.

4. Lakoff (2007), 138.

5. Wayne LaPierre, *Guns, Freedom and Terrorism* (Nashville: WND Books, 2003), 12.

6. LaPierre 54-55.

7. LaPierre 61.

8. LaPierre 145-146.

9. Wayne LaPierre interview with Gloria Borger and Bob Schieffer, *Face the Nation*, April 25, 1999.

10. LaPierre (2003), 192.

11. LaPierre 192..

12. LaPierre 193.

13. Hannah Arendt, *On Revolution* (New York: Penguin Books, 1963), 40

14. Michael C. Dorf, "Federal Court Of Appeals Says The Second Amendment Places Limits On Gun Control Legislation," FindLaw, Oct 31, 2001, http://writ.news.findlaw.com/dorf/20011031.html.

15. Jered Townsend, "Gun Control From Michigan," YouTube, July 23, 2007, http://www.youtube.com/watch?v=ZqrpjLZJVu4.

16. Jim Schaefer and Julie Hinds, "Weapons Enthusiast Takes Aim At Candidates," *Detroit Free Press*, July 25, 2007.

17. "NRA, Democrats Team Up To Pass Gun Bill," June 13, 2007, http://www.cbsnews.com/stories/2007/06/13/politics/main2923101.shtml

18. Jeffery (2007).

3. Death By Immigration

1. Patrick Buchanan interviewed by Neil Cavuto, *Your World With Neil Cavuto*, August 25, 2006.

2. Patrick Buchanan, "Republican National Convention Speech," Houston, Texas, August 17, 1992, http://www.buchanan.org/pa-92-0817-rnc.html.

3. Carl von Clausewitz, *On War* (New York: Oxford University Press, 2007). The translation from the German used here is from George Lakoff, "Metaphor and War," Peace Research 23 (1991):25-32.

4. Lakoff 26.

5. Patrick Buchanan, "Announcement Speech," Manchester Institute of Arts and Sciences, Manchester, NH, March 20, 1995, http://www.buchanan.org/pa-95-0320-announce.html.

6. Patrick Buchanan, *Death Of The West* (New York: St. Martin's Press, 2002), 24.

7. Buchanan 62-63.

8. Buchanan 94.

9. Buchanan 147.

10. S. P. Huntington, "Clash of Civilizations?" *Foreign Affairs* 72:3 (1993), 22-49.

11. Huntington 22.

12. S. P. Huntington, "Reconsidering Immigration: Is Mexico a Special Case?" Backgrounder, Center for Immigration Studies, Nov 2000, 5. Cited in *The Death Of The West*, 126, and *State of Emergency*, 136

13. Jake Tapper, "Buchanan, McCain Go Head-To-Head: GOP presidential hopefuls debate whether U.S. had any business stopping Hitler." 23 Sep 1999, *Salon.com*, http://www.salon.com/news/feature/1999/09/23/buchanan.

14. Buchanan (2002), 88.

15. Patrick J. Buchanan, "The Recantation of Dr. Watson," October 30, 2007, http://www.worldnetdaily.com/news/article.asp?ARTICLE_ID=58410.

16. Enoch Powell, "Like the Roman, I see the River Tiber foaming with much blood," April 20, 1968, EnochPowell.com, http://www.enochpowell.com/Rivers-of-Blood-Speech-Enoch-Powell.html.

17. David Sirota, *Hostile Takeover: How Big Money And Corruption Conquered Our Government—And How We Take It Back* (New York: Crown, 2006).

18. Sally Kohn, "Migration and Corn," *The Huffington Post*, 18 May 07, http://www.huffingtonpost.com/sally-kohn/migration-and-corn_b_48801.html.

19. Sherrod Brown, *Myths of Free Trade: Why American Trade Policy Has Failed* (New York: New Press, 2004), 21.

20. Pat Choate, *Agents of Influence* (New York: Simon & Schuster, 1990).

21. Paul Krugman, 'Trouble With Trade,' *New York Times* December, 28, 2007, http://www.nytimes.com/2007/12/28/opinion/28krugman.html.

4. Lots Of 9/11's

1. IAEA refers to the "International Atomic Energy Agency."

2. John MacArthur and Ann Coulter interviewed by Sean Hannity and Alan Colmes, *Hannity & Colmes*, October 13, 2003.

3. David Daley, "Spin On The Right Ann Coulter: Lights' All Shining On Her," *Hartford Courant,* June 25, 1999.

4. Michael Isikoff, *Uncovering Clinton: A Reporter's Story* (New York, Three Rivers Press, 1999), 184.

5. Isikoff 184-185.

6. F. J. Murray, "Is This The President's 'Distinguishing Characteristic'? *Washington Times*, October 15, 1997, A(2):A1.

7. Ann Coulter interviewed by Geraldo Rivera, *Rivera Live*, Oct 15, 1997.

8. Ann Coulter, "This is War," *National Review Online*, Sep 13, 2001, http://www.nationalreview.com/coulter/coulter.shtml.

9. Coulter 2001.

10. Jonah Goldberg, "L'Affaire Coulter," *National Review Online*, October 1, 2001, http://article.nationalreview.com/?q=MmVhMGI5NGFjZjIxMjBmMTE5N2FlYzgzNGFmZTYzZGQ=.

11. Ann Coulter, *Treason: Liberal Treachery From the Cold War to the War On Terrorism* (New York: Crown Forum), 1.

12. Coulter 43-44.

13. Coulter 155.

14. Coulter 155.

15. Coulter 292.

16. Coulter 286-286.

17. John Dewey, *The Political Writings* (Indianapolis: Hackett Publishing, 1993), 241.

18. Dewey 243.

19. John F. Kennedy, "Message of Senator John F. Kennedy to the Nation's New Voters," October 5, 1960. For a full text of this speech see, The American Presidency Project, http://www.presidency.ucsb.edu/ws/?pid=60424.

20. Richard M. Nixon, "Statement by the Vice President of the United States, Peace Corps," November 6, 1960. For a full text of this speech see, The American Presidency Project, http://www.presidency.ucsb.edu/ws/?pid=25327.

21. Dewey (1993), 215.

22. Dewey 217.

5. The Billy Club

1. Geraldo Rivera interviewed by Bill O'Reilly, *The O'Reilly Factor*,

April 5, 2005.

2. Al Franken, *Lies And The Lying Liars Who Tell Them: A Fair And Balanced Look At The Right* (New York: Dutton Adult, 2003) 67.

3. This incident took place between Bill O'Reilly and Al Franken on CSPAN's *BookTV*, Jun 3, 2003.

4. "Bill O'Reilly Shouts Down Al Franken," YouTube.com, http://www.youtube.com/watch?v=fpOSgT-osHk.

5. Bill O'Reilly, *Culture Warrior* (New York: Broadway, 2006), 1.

6. O'Reilly 3-4.

7. O'Reilly 13.

8. O'Reilly 16.

9. O'Reilly 16-17.

10. O'Reilly 33.

11. O'Reilly 35.

12. Byron York, "Soros Funded Stewart Defense,' *National Review Online*, February 17, 2005, http://www.nationalreview.com/york/york200502170843.asp.

13. "O'Reilly: Media Matters, Daily Kos, MoveOn "lead intimidators" of Democratic presidential candidates," Media Matters for America, July 31, 2007, http://mediamatters.org/items/printable/200707310007.

14. O'Reilly (2006), 2.

15. O'Reilly 104.

16. O'Reilly 106.

17. O'Reilly 106.

18. O'Reilly 123.

19. O'Reilly 113.

20. Richard Rorty, *Achieving Our Country: Leftist Thought in Twentieth-Century America* (Cambridge: Harvard University Press, 1998), 81.

21. Michael Eric Dyson interviewed by Bill Maher, *Real Time With Bill Maher*, September 30, 2007.

22. Theodore Adorno, *The Authoritarian Personality* (New York: Harper, 1950).

23. Lewis Filler, *The Muckrakers* (Stanford: Stanford University Press, 1968), 61.

24. Thomas Lawson, *Frenzied Finance* (New York: Ridgeway-Thayer, 1905), vii.

25. See, Ida Tarbell, *The History of the Standard Oil Company* (New York: Peter Smith, 1904), Upton Sinclair, *The Jungle* (New York: The Jungle Publication Co., 1906), Ralph Nader, *Unsafe At Any Speed: The Designed-In Dangers Of The American Automobile* (New York: Grossman, 1965), Barbara Ehrenreich, *Nickel and Dimed: On (Not) Getting By In America* (New York: Metropolitan Books, 2001).

6. Christmas Killers

1. Jerry Falwell interviewed by Joe Scarborough, *Scarborough Country*, November 28, 2003.

2. Liberty Counsel "Friend or Foe" Christmas Campaign. The web site associated with the campaign lists some resources freely available for download; quoted passage from a linked PDF file titled, "sample full page ad to use in local newspaper," http://lc.org/helpsavechristmas/index.htm, site accessed: January 1, 2008.

3. Jerry Falwell interviewed by John Kasich, *The O'Reilly Factor*, Nov 23, 2005.

4. Henry Ford, *The International Jew: The World's Foremost Problem* (Dearborn: The Dearborn Publishing Company, 1920-1922), 269.

5. John Gibson, *The War On Christmas: How The Liberal Plot To Ban The Sacred Christian Holiday Is Worse Than You Thought* (New York: Sentinel, 2005), xxii.

6. Gibson xxii.

7. Gibson xxii-xxiv.

8. John Gibson, *The Big Story With John Gibson*, Oct 21, 2005.

9. Gibson (2005), 196.

10. Gibson 113.

11. Gibson 55.

12. Gibson 86.

13. Gibson 109-110.

14. Gibson 90.

15. Gibson 163.

16. Raymond Williams, *Keywords: A Vocabulary of Culture and Society* (New York: Oxford University Press, 1976), p. 87.

7. Child Of Pain

1. *Hannity & Colmes*, Aug 23, 2004.

2. *Hannity & Colmes*, Jun 2, 2003.

3. U.S. Department of Justice, Attorney General's Commission On Pornography: Final Report, 1986, http://www.porn-report.com.

4. James Dobson, *Marriage Under Fire: Why We Must Win This Battle* (New York: Tyndale House Publishers, 2007), 41.

5. Dobson 8.

6. Dobson 4.

7. James Dobson, *Dare To Discipline* (Carol Stream, IL: Tyndale House Publishers, 1992), 39.

8. Dobson 23-24.

9. Dobson 28.

10. Dobson 28-29.

11. Dobson 35.

12. Dobson 36.

13. Dobson 22.

14. Dobson 34.

15. James Dobson, *Bringing Up Boys,* (Carol Stream, IL: Tyndale House Publishers, 2001), 113-130.

16. Interview with Joseph Nicolosi, "The Compassionate Answer," *San Francisco Faith: The Bay Areas Lay Catholic Newspaper*, Vol. 2 No. 7, July-August 1998, http://www.ldolphin.org/narth2.html

17. James Dobson, "Can Homosexuality Be Treated And Prevented?" *Focus On The Family Newsletter*, 2007, http://www.focusonthefamily.com/docstudy/newsletters/A000000264.cfm

18. Dobson.

19. September 22 – 24, Omni Shoreham Hotel, Washington, DC.

20. Dobson 2007,

21. Dobson 2007.

22. Alexis de Tocqueville, *Democracy in America*, ed. J.P. Maier, trans. George Lawrence, (Garden City, N.Y.: Anchor Books, 1969), 513-17.

23. Arendt 1963, 158-159.

24. Lyndon Johnson, "Remarks at the Signing of the Water Quality Act of 1965," October 2, 1965, American Presidency Project, http://www.presidency.ucsb.edu/ws/index.php?pid=27289&st=landsca pe&st1=.

25. Al Gore, *An Inconvenient Truth: The Planetary Emergency of Global Warming and What We Can Do About It* (New York: Rodale Books, 2006), 289.

26. Arendt 1963, 118-120.

27. Thomas Jefferson, "First Inaugural Address," Washington, D.C., March 5, 1801, http://www.bartleby.com/124/pres16.html.

8. The War Against The War

1. Dinesh D'Souza, *Your World With Neil Cavuto*, February 9, 2007.

2. Dinesh D'Souza, *The Factor*, February 16, 2007.

3. D'Souza.

4. Dinesh D'Souza, *Letters To A Young Conservative* (New York: Basic Books, 2002).

5. Dinesh D'Souza, *The Enemy at Home* (New York: Doubleday, 2007), 58.

6. D'Souza 59.

7. D'Souza 17.

8. D'Souza 95-96.

9. Osama Bin Laden, 'Letter to America,' *Guardian Unlimited*, November 24, 2002, http://observer.guardian.co.uk/worldview/sto-

ry/0,,845725,00.html

    10. Bin Laden.

    11. D'Souza 2007, 1.

    12. D'Souza 269-270.

    13. D'Souza 270.

    14. D'Souza xiii.

    15. Abraham Lincoln, "The Perpetuation of Our Political Institutions," January 27, 1838, TeachingAmericanHistory.org, http://teachingamericanhistory.org/library/index.asp?document=157.

    16. D'Souza 2007, 58.

    17. Seymour Hirsch," Annals of National Security: Torture At Abu Ghraib," *The New Yorker,* May 10, 2007.

    18. D'Souza 2007, 138.

    19. D'Souza 139.

    20. D'Souza 140.

    21. D'Souza 166.

    22. D'Souza 171.

    23. D'Souza 171-172.

    24. D'Souza 187.

    25. John Kiriakou interviewed by John Roberts, *CNN American Morning,* December 11, 2007, http://transcripts.cnn.com/TRANSCRIPTS/0712/11/ltm.03.html.

9. The Return of Pragmatism

    1. Arendt 1969, 12.

    2. Newt Gingrich, *Winning the Future: A 21st Century Contract With America* (Washington, DC: Regnery Publishing, Inc., 2006), 1.

    3. Rudolph Giuliani, *Leadership* (New York: Hyperion, 2002), 5.

    4. John Elster, *Deliberative Democracy* (Cambridge: Cambridge University Press, 1998), 19-21.

    5. Diana C. Mutz, *Hearing the Other Side: Deliberative Versus Participatory Democracy,* (Cambridge: Cambridge University Press, 2006), 4.

6. An example of this mistake can be found in the work of libertarian TV pundit, Lou Dobbs' book, *The War on the Middle Class: How the Government, Big Business, and Special Interest Groups Are Waging War on the American Dream and How to Fight Back*, (New York: Viking, 2007), 197.

7. Jürgen Habermas, T*he Structural Transformation of the Public Square: An Inquiry Into A Category Of Bourgeois Society* (Cambridge: MIT Press, 1989), 30-32.

8. Habermas 65.

9. Habermas 186.

10. Dewey 1993, 216.

11. A. O. Hirschman, "On Democracy In Latin America," *The New York Review Of Books*, April 10, 1986.

12. Orwell 1984, 119.

13. William James, *Pragmatism: A New Way For Some Old Ways Of Thinking* (New York: Longmans, Green and Co.,1907), 45.

14. World Watch Institute, "Global War on Global Warming Heats Up," August 1, 2002, http://www.worldwatch.org/node/1733.

15. Dobbs 2007.

16. Dobbs 197.

17. John Yoo, *War By Other Means: An Insider's Account of the War on Terror*, New York: Atlantic Monthly Press, 2006, 120.

18. Orwell 1993, 120.